Mary Engelbreit's

FAN

FARE

cookbook

120 slow cooker recipe favorites

Other cookbooks from Mary Engelbreit

Mary Engelbreit's Queen of the Kitchen Cookbook

Mary Engelbreit's Sweet Treats Dessert Cookbook

*Mary Engelbreit's Fan Fare Cookbook:
120 Family Favorite Recipes*

Mary Engelbreit's

FARE

cookbook

120 slow cooker recipe favorites

Illustrated by
Mary Engelbreit

Recipes by Friends and Fans

**Andrews McMeel
Publishing, LLC**
Kansas City • Sydney • London

Library of Congress Control Number: 2010927040

Contents

If my family had to depend
on me for food,
they would starve to death
in a really cute kitchen.

—Mary Engelbreit

Letter from Mary

It's no secret that I'm not the chef in our family! And even though I do not devote my time to cooking, I still love and appreciate good food. For this cookbook, I called upon my family, friends, and fans for their favorite slow cooker meals, and, boy, did they deliver! Here you'll find recipes for chilis, soups, and stews, as well as hearty beef, chicken, and pork dishes, delicious sides, dips, and sauces, and even a few delectable desserts. All are easy and exceptionally delicious and, best of all, since you can "set it and forget it" you won't have to devote a lot of time to cooking!

Of course, we here at the Mary Engelbreit Studio tested everything in our kitchen to ensure each recipe's measurements, steps, and delectability!

I hope you enjoy these recipes as much as we have.

Let's get cooking!

Mary

P.S. Cooking times may vary among slow cooker makes and models. These recipes were tested with newer models, which cook faster. Consult your manufacturer's instructions and adjust times as needed.

Chili is much improved
by having had a day
to contemplate its fate.

—John Steele Gordon

Chilis

Vivian Chaplin
Deltona, Florida

Best-Ever Chili

Makes 4 to 6 servings

1 pound ground beef

1 (15-ounce) can tomato sauce

1 (15-ounce) can red kidney beans, with liquid

1 (15-ounce) can pinto beans, with liquid

1 (15-ounce) can spicy chili beans, with liquid

1/2 cup diced onion

1/4 cup canned diced green chiles

1/4 cup diced celery

1/2 cup drained jarred fried peppers (such as Mancini
    brand) or pepperoncini, diced

1 (10-ounce) can beef consommé

1 (28-ounce) can diced tomatoes, with liquid

1 teaspoon ground cumin

2 tablespoons chili powder

1 teaspoon black pepper

1 teaspoon salt

Brown the meat well in a skillet over medium-high heat, using a fork to crumble the meat into pea-size pieces, 8 to 10 minutes; drain off the fat. Combine the meat with the rest of the ingredients in a 6-quart slow cooker. Cover and cook on low for 7 to 8 hours. Serve with corn bread and/or crackers or over elbow macaroni as chili mac. ■

I have been searching for the Best Ever Chili recipe for many years and have finally found it! Try it and see for yourself. —UC

Brandon Hieber
Chicago, Illinois

Tomatillo & Steak
Chili

Makes 4 to 6 servings

1 tablespoon vegetable oil (or vegetable oil spray)

1 1/2 pounds beef stew meat, cut into medium dice

Salt and black pepper

1 large yellow onion, cut into small dice

1 green bell pepper, cut into small dice

12 fresh tomatillos, husked and cut into medium dice

4 cloves garlic, chopped

1/2 cup white wine

1 (28-ounce) can whole peeled tomatoes, with liquid

2 (15-ounce) cans black beans, drained and rinsed

1 (15-ounce) can spicy chili beans, with liquid

1 (15-ounce) can mild chili beans, with liquid

1 tablespoon ground cumin, or to taste

1 tablespoon chili powder, or to taste

2 (12-ounce) cans whole tomatillos (available at Mexican
        food stores or in the Mexican food section of
        supermarkets), drained and rinsed

1/4 cup chopped fresh cilantro

2 ripe avocados

1/2 cup water

Put the oil in a skillet and sauté the meat over medium heat, seasoning with salt and pepper, until golden brown. Drain off the grease and set the meat aside. In the same pan, sauté the onion, bell pepper, fresh tomatillos, and garlic until tender, 10 to 15 minutes. Deglaze the pan with the white wine, scraping up any stuck bits of food.

Put the browned meat and the contents of the pan into a 6-quart slow cooker and stir in the canned tomatoes, beans, cumin, and chili powder. Puree the drained canned tomatillos in a blender until smooth. Add to the chili along with the cilantro. Stir well, cover, bring to a boil on high heat, then reduce the heat to low. Keep simmering, occasionally checking the seasoning and adding salt and pepper as needed, for about 7 hours. Check the seasoning, and cook for another 30 minutes.

Before serving, peel and pit the avocados and puree them with the water in the blender. Add to the chili. Check the seasonings once more; don't be afraid to add another pinch of cumin and chili powder. ■

chilis

Theresa Norsky
Cohocton, New York

Grandmama Wynne's
Fall Foliage Chili

Makes 10 to 12 servings

1 pound ground beef

3 medium onions, cut into large chunks or half rings

3 to 5 cloves garlic, minced

1 tablespoon olive oil, if needed

1 teaspoon salt

1 teaspoon black pepper

1 to 2 teaspoons chili powder, to taste

1/2 to 1 teaspoon cayenne, to taste

1/2 to 1 teaspoon paprika, to taste

2 tablespoons cider vinegar

1/4 cup loosely packed brown sugar

3 (15-ounce) cans dark red kidney beans, with liquid

3 (15-ounce) cans light red kidney beans, with liquid

3 (15-ounce) cans diced tomatoes, with liquid

1 (12-ounce) can tomato paste

1 cup sour cream, milk, or cream, plus more for topping
        (optional)

Grated cheddar cheese, for topping (optional)

Cook the ground beef, onions, and garlic in a large skillet
or sauté pan over medium-high heat, using a small amount
of olive oil to prevent sticking if the meat is very lean, until

the meat is browned and the onions are tender, about 8 to 10 minutes. Transfer the mixture to a 5-quart slow cooker. Add the salt, black pepper, chili powder, cayenne, paprika, vinegar, brown sugar, beans, diced tomatoes, and tomato paste. Cover and let stew on low all day or for at least 6 hours. About 15 minutes before serving, stir in the sour cream, milk, or cream until well incorporated. Don't cook the chili too long after that or it might scorch. If the chili seems too thick (and I don't think there is such a thing), you can add water to thin it down. ■

Every October our town has a Fall Foliage Festival, complete with a tree-sitting contest. As family and friends gather together to celebrate, a pot of chili in the slow cooker means we can go to the festival off and on all weekend, returning home to warm up with chili. The chili's taste becomes richer if there's any left over for the next day. But be careful in the reheating, as the milk will make it burn fairly quickly. Personally, I use the microwave to reheat and have never had the chili burn. —JM

Jenny Matlock
Mesa, Arizona

Green Chile Stew

Makes 6 servings

2 teaspoons olive oil

2 pounds lean beef stew meat or 2 pounds boneless chicken, light or dark meat, cubed

Vegetable oil cooking spray

2 cups chopped fresh green chiles

1 cup chopped onion

2 cups cubed potatoes

1 (14-ounce) can beef or chicken broth

1/2 teaspoon salt

1/2 teaspoon black pepper

1/2 teaspoon garlic powder

Flour or corn tortillas, for serving (optional)

Sour cream, grated cheddar cheese, sliced green onions, chopped fresh cilantro, and crumbled tortilla chips, for serving

Heat the oil in a large skillet over medium-high heat and brown the meat on all sides, 8 to 10 minutes. While the meat is cooking, set a 5-quart slow cooker to low and spray the inside of the cooker with nonstick cooking spray. Put the meat into the slow cooker and lightly brown the chiles and onion in the same skillet, about 5 minutes. Add the chiles and onion to the slow cooker along with all the remaining ingredients except the garnishes and tortillas. Cover and cook 7 to 8 hours.

If you wish to use tortillas with the stew, wrap them tightly in aluminum foil about 30 minutes before the end of the cooking time. Put the foil-wrapped pack on the lid of the slow cooker and turn occasionally to warm and soften the tortillas. Serve with sour cream, cheddar cheese, green onions, cilantro, and crumbled tortilla chips. ■

My family loves this stew. Both beef and chicken are excellent, and I almost always serve the warmed tortillas alongside the stew. It's fun serving a variety of the garnishes so each person can customize the stew to taste. —JM

chilis

Kristi Zimmerman
Centennial, Colorado

Aunt Diane's Chili

Makes 6 to 8 servings

1/2 pound dried pinto or kidney beans

1 quart water

2 pounds lean ground beef chuck or round

1 1/2 cups chopped onion

2 cloves garlic, minced

1 (28-ounce) can diced tomatoes, with liquid

1 green bell pepper, chopped

1/2 teaspoon hot red pepper flakes

1 tablespoon chili powder

2 teaspoons salt

1 teaspoon ground cumin

Simmer the beans in 3 cups of the water for 30 minutes. Let stand, covered, for 2 hours, until softened; drain. Brown the meat in a large skillet over medium-high heat, 8 to 10 minutes. Put the beans, meat, and remaining ingredients (including the last cup of water) in a 5-quart slow cooker. Cover and cook on low for 8 to 10 hours or on high for 3 to 4 hours. ■

We often serve it with grated cheese, sour cream, and crackers. Also tastes good with a chewy artisan bread.

—KZ

Stephanie Jonker
Shreveport, Louisiana

Aunt Jane's Chili

Makes 8 to 10 servings

1 1/2 pounds ground beef

1/4 to 1/2 pound bulk sausage

1/2 pound beef stew meat, chopped

1 small onion, chopped

1 small green bell pepper, chopped

1/2 (2 1/2-ounce) jar chopped mushrooms, drained

1 (15-ounce) can pinto beans, with liquid

1 (15-ounce) can pinto beans with jalapeños, with liquid

1 (1-ounce) packet chili seasoning

1 (15-ounce) can stewed tomatoes

Brown the meats with the onion and green pepper in a large skillet over medium-high heat, 12 to 15 minutes. Drain, then transfer to a 5-quart slow cooker and add the mushrooms, beans, chili seasoning, and stewed tomatoes. Mix well, cover, and cook on low for 7 to 8 hours, stirring occasionally. Serve with crackers or corn bread. ■

This is a fairly mild chili. You could give it some zing with 1 teaspoon cayenne pepper. —SJ

chilis

Patti Hurley
Martinsville, New Jersey

Warm You Up Chili

Makes 8 to 10 servings

1 1/2 pounds ground beef, turkey, or chicken

1 (28-ounce) can crushed tomatoes, with liquid

2 medium onions, chopped

1 large green bell pepper, chopped

2 medium stalks celery, chopped

2 (15-ounce) cans red or white kidney beans, with liquid

4 beef bouillon cubes

2 teaspoons chili powder

1 teaspoon ground cumin

Dash of hot red pepper flakes (optional)

1 cup drained canned or frozen corn (optional)

Shredded cheddar cheese and sour cream, for serving

Brown the meat in a skillet over medium-high heat, 10 to 12 minutes. Drain and transfer it to a 5-quart slow cooker. Add the tomatoes, onions, green pepper, celery, beans, bouillon cubes, chili powder, cumin, and hot pepper flakes and mix. Cover and cook on low for 7 to 8 hours or on high for 2 to 3 hours. If desired, add the corn during the last 30 minutes of cooking. Serve with the cheese and sour cream. ■

$\mathcal{T}$his is a great party recipe, with a variety of toppings
for each guest to choose from.
A side of corn bread and a salad are all you need
for a great and easy meal. —PH

Carrie Shindorf
Cosby, Missouri

Pork Chili

Makes 4 to 6 servings

2 to 2 1/2 pounds cubed pork loin or lean pork shoulder

2 tablespoons vegetable oil

1 (28-ounce) can diced tomatoes, with liquid

1 (15-ounce) can chili beans, with liquid

1 (8-ounce) can tomato sauce

1/2 cup salsa

1/2 cup chopped onion

1 small bell pepper, chopped

1 tablespoon chili powder

Minced jalapeño or other hot chile (optional)

1 clove garlic, minced

Salt and black pepper

1/4 teaspoon hot red pepper flakes, or to taste

Flour tortillas, for serving

Brown the pork cubes in the hot oil in a large skillet over medium heat, 10 minutes. Drain. Place the pork in a 5-quart slow cooker and add the tomatoes, beans, tomato sauce, salsa, onion, bell pepper, chili powder, jalapeño to taste, garlic, salt and pepper to taste, and red pepper flakes. Cover and cook on low for 7 to 8 hours. Serve with the tortillas. ■

Denise Shuman
Laurel, Mississippi

White Chili

Makes 6 to 8 servings

2 cups cooked shredded or chopped chicken meat

1 (15-ounce) can corn, drained

1 (15-ounce) can navy beans, drained and rinsed

1 (15-ounce) can seasoned diced tomatoes, such as
Del Monte's Green Pepper and Onion, or your
favorite flavor

1 (10-ounce) can condensed cream of mushroom soup

1 (4-ounce) can sliced mushrooms, drained

1 (14-ounce) can chicken broth (not condensed)

Hot sauce

Combine all the ingredients, including hot sauce to taste, in a 4-quart slow cooker, cover, and cook on low for 6 to 8 hours or high for 2 to 3 hours. ■

I just love this recipe! I always have the ingredients in my pantry. You can use canned or leftover chicken or veggies or use spicy beans or tomatoes (and skip the hot sauce)—whatever you have on hand.

—DS

chilis

23

Mylene Powell
Miami, Florida

Vegetarian Chili

Makes 8 servings

1 teaspoon olive oil

1 (12-ounce) package Morningstar Farms Meal Starters
       Grillers Recipe Crumbles, thawed

1 onion, chopped

2 tablespoons minced garlic

2 tablespoons salt

2 tablespoons black pepper

1 1/2 cups vegetable stock

1 (15-ounce) can diced tomatoes, with liquid

1 (15-ounce) can dark red kidney beans, drained

1 (15-ounce) can chili beans, drained

1 tablespoon plus 1 teaspoon Tabasco sauce

2 tablespoons chili powder

1 teaspoon cayenne

1 tablespoon brown sugar

2 cups shredded sharp cheddar cheese

Combine the olive oil, Crumbles, onion, garlic, salt, and black pepper in a large skillet over medium-high heat and cook until the onion is tender, 10 minutes. Transfer to a 4-quart slow cooker. Add the stock, tomatoes, beans, Tabasco, chili powder, and cayenne, cover, and cook on low for 2 to 5 hours. Add the brown sugar and stir. Serve by itself or with cooked rice, garnished with the cheddar cheese. ∎

The recipe is quick, easy, and tastes great—
meat eaters have not been able to tell the difference.
Great for camping trips; easy for parties
(nachos with chili and cheese).
Healthy and low-fat. —MP

Carmela Mazurco
Shelby Township, Michigan

Vegetable Chili

Makes 8 servings

1/4 cup olive oil

2 or 3 large zucchini, cubed

2 medium onions, diced

1 red bell pepper, cubed

1 yellow bell pepper, cubed

2 or 3 medium potatoes, peeled and cubed

2 large carrots, grated

4 stalks celery, sliced

3 or 4 cloves roasted garlic or 3 cloves raw garlic, minced

2 (28-ounce) cans fire-roasted crushed tomatoes or regular
    crushed tomatoes, with liquid

1 (15-ounce) can black beans, with liquid

1 teaspoon sugar

1/2 teaspoon cayenne, or to taste

1 (1-ounce) package chili seasoning

2 tablespoons chili powder

1 teaspoon dried oregano

1 bay leaf

Heat the oil in a large skillet or sauté pan over medium-high heat and sauté the zucchini, onions, bell peppers, potatoes, carrots, and celery until slightly softened, 5 to 10 minutes. Transfer these ingredients to a 6-quart slow cooker and add the garlic, tomatoes, beans, sugar, cayenne, chili seasoning, chili powder, oregano, and bay leaf. Cover and simmer on low for 7 to 8 hours, until everything is cooked through. Remove the bay leaf before serving. ■

Since my husband has gout, he tries to stay away from high-protein foods. He loves chili, but between the beans and the meat, it was too much protein in one meal. So I revised my chili recipe to exclude the meat but keep its original flavor. This recipe can be done on top of the stove (30 to 40 minutes) or in a slow cooker, and it can be served alone or with rice. —CM

chilis

Good manners:
The noise you don't make
when you're eating soup.

—Bennett Cerf

Soups & Stews

Wendy Mahonen

Uncasville, Connecticut

Best Beef Stew

Makes 4 to 6 servings

1/4 cup all-purpose flour

1/4 teaspoon salt

1/4 teaspoon black pepper

2 pounds beef stew meat (chuck is best), cubed

1 1/3 cups water

1 (10-ounce) can beef broth

1 clove garlic, minced (about 1/2 teaspoon)

1 (1.5-ounce) packet hearty beef stew seasoning for
    slow cookers

1 (10-ounce) can condensed cream of mushroom soup

 4 to 6 medium Yukon Gold potatoes, peeled and cut into
        1-inch cubes

1 cup baby carrots, 1/2 cup thinly sliced, 1/2 cup left whole

1 small white onion, diced (about 1/4 cup)

Mix the flour, salt, and black pepper in a small bowl. Toss the cubed beef in the flour mixture to coat thoroughly and set aside.

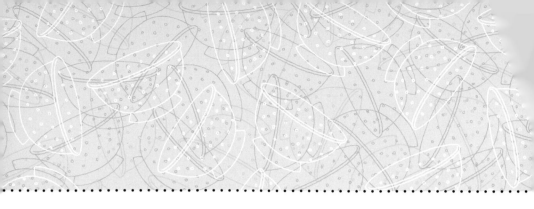

In a small bowl, combine the water, beef broth, garlic, and hearty beef stew seasoning. Mix well and then stir in the cream of mushroom soup until blended thoroughly.

Place the beef cubes, potatoes, carrots, and onion in a 5-quart slow cooker and stir to mix the beef and vegetables together. Pour your sauce/gravy mixture over the top of the beef and vegetables and mix well. Cover and cook on low for 7 to 8 hours or on high for 3 to 4 hours (I've tried both, and the stew tastes perfect using either temperature/time). ◼

I've tried many slow cooker beef stew recipes over the past few years, and I had yet to find one that I really liked. After doing quite a bit of experimentation with simple and complicated recipes, this one seems to be the easiest and the most flavorful beef stew recipe (I've ever done)! The beef tastes so tender, and the potatoes just melt in your mouth. —WM

soups & stews

Joni Matthews
Saint Augustine, Florida

Mouthwatering
Beef Stew

Makes 6 servings

2 tablespoons extra virgin olive oil

2 pounds beef stew meat, cut into small pieces

1 large onion

5 potatoes, peeled and diced

2 (14-ounce) cans sliced carrots or other vegetable, drained

1 (8-ounce) can tomato sauce

1 teaspoon vinegar

1 cup sugar

1/2 teaspoon salt

1/2 teaspoon black pepper

1 tablespoon minced garlic

Set a 6-quart slow cooker on high. Put the olive oil in the bottom. Add the meat, then the onion, potatoes, and carrots. Pour the tomato sauce over the top. Then add the vinegar, sugar, salt, pepper, and garlic. Cover and cook on high for about 20 minutes. Then turn the heat down to low and cook for 7 to 8 hours. The tomato sauce with the sugar will form a wonderful gravy for your meat. This dish will make your whole house smell delightful. ■

Lissa Coulter
Garner, North Carolina

Beefy Stew

Makes 6 servings

2 pounds beef stew meat, cut into 1-inch cubes

2 to 3 tablespoons all-purpose flour (optional)

1 onion, thickly sliced

1 (1-ounce) envelope onion soup mix

1 pound baby potatoes, whole, or red potatoes, cubed

1 (16-ounce) bag baby carrots (preferably extra petite)

2 (10-ounce) cans condensed tomato soup

1 loaf crusty herb (artisan) bread, for serving (optional)

Coat the beef cubes in flour if desired. Layer the ingredients in a 6-quart slow cooker with the onion slices on the bottom; the meat, onion soup mix, potatoes, and carrots in the middle; and the condensed tomato soup covering the top. Cover and cook on low until the vegetables are tender, 6 to 8 hours (but it will do fine for up to 10 hours), or on high for about 4 hours. Serve with crusty herb bread. ■

If I need to set more places at the dinner table,
this recipe is easily doubled for a crowd,
and leftovers freeze well, too. —LC

soups & stews

Jennifer Mills
Bloomington, Indiana

Savory Stew

Makes 4 servings

1 1/2 pounds beef stew meat, cubed

2 large potatoes, peeled and cubed

1 pound carrots, sliced

1 large onion, sliced

2 stalks celery, chopped

1 pound mushrooms, sliced

1 (6-ounce) can tomato paste

1 tablespoon cornstarch

1/2 cup water

1 tablespoon caraway seeds

1 teaspoon garlic powder

1 teaspoon paprika

1 tablespoon salt

1 tablespoon black pepper

Mix everything in a 6-quart slow cooker, cover, and cook for 8 to 10 hours. Can be served over hot noodles. ■

Susan McDonald
Mabelvale, Arkansas

Southwest Soup

Makes 6 to 8 servings

2 pounds lean ground beef

2 (15-ounce) cans stewed tomatoes (Mexican recipe if
  available), with liquid

1 (10-ounce) can diced tomatoes with green chiles

1 (15-ounce) can whole kernel corn

3 (15-ounce) cans beans of your choosing (my family likes
  2 cans pinto beans and 1 can black beans)

1 (6-ounce) jar sliced mushrooms

1 (1-ounce) envelope taco seasoning mix

1 (1-ounce) envelope dry ranch dressing mix

Shredded cheese (Mexican or Fiesta blend if available),
  for garnish

Tortilla chips (scoop-style work very well), for serving

Brown the ground beef in a large skillet over medium-high heat and drain, 10 minutes. Empty all the cans into a 5-quart slow cooker. (Do NOT drain!) Add the seasoning and dressing mixes and ground beef, mixing well. Cover and cook on low for 4 to 6 hours or on high for 2 to 3 hours until heated through. Sprinkle with cheese and serve with tortilla chips. ■

soups & stews

JoAnne Davis
Springfield, Illinois

Jo's Sweet-and-Sour
Beef Stew
with Dumplings

Makes 4 to 6 servings

1 to 1 1/2 pounds beef stew meat, cut into bite-sized pieces

1 red or Vidalia onion, thinly sliced and separated
        into rings

1 pound carrots, cut into 1/2- to 1-inch pieces

1 pound potatoes, peeled and cut into eighths

1 (15-ounce) can tomato sauce

1/2 can plus 2/3 cup water

2/3 cup firmly packed dark brown sugar

1/3 cup apple cider vinegar, red wine vinegar, or
        light balsamic vinegar

1/4 teaspoon celery seeds

Garlic salt

Black pepper

2 tablespoons cornstarch

1 can refrigerated buttermilk biscuits (5- or 10-biscuit size,
        depending on the diameter of your slow cooker)

1 (16-ounce) bag wide noodles

1 tablespoon butter (optional)

Combine the meat, onion, carrots, potatoes, tomato sauce,
1/2 tomato sauce can of water, the brown sugar, vinegar,

celery seeds, garlic salt, and pepper to taste in a 5-quart slow cooker. Cover and cook on high for 1 hour, then on low for 4 to 6 hours, until the carrots and potatoes are fork-tender.

When done, combine the 2/3 cup water and the cornstarch, stir the mixture into the stew, and turn the heat to high. Arrange the biscuits across the top of the stew, sides touching, to make easy dumplings. Cook for about 15 minutes, covered, until the biscuits have risen and are no longer sticky to the touch.

While the biscuits are cooking, cook the noodles according to the package directions. Drain. If desired, add the butter to the noodles after draining to keep them from sticking. Serve the stew and dumplings over the noodles. ■

This recipe is one I started making back in the late seventies. It's not a traditional sweet-and-sour sauce, but it has that taste. Everyone I have made it for over the years has really enjoyed it, and they comment on how unusual it is to be called a beef stew. —JD

soups & stews

Jan Lipinski
Houston, Texas

Slovenian Stew

Makes 6 servings

2 tablespoons olive oil

1 pound beef stew meat, cubed

1 small to medium onion, chopped

1 (10-ounce) can condensed tomato soup

3 cans water

1/2 teaspoon paprika

Salt and black pepper

1 cup barley

3/4 cup sour cream

Heat the olive oil in a large skillet over medium-high heat and cook the meat and onion until the meat is browned on two sides, about 10 minutes. In a bowl, stir the tomato soup and water. Add the paprika and salt and pepper. Fold in the barley. Stir and dump into a 4-quart slow cooker along with the meat and onion. Cover and cook on high for at least 3 1/2 hours or low for 6 hours. Ladle it into a big bowl, slowly stir in the sour cream, and serve. ■

I grew up on Lake Erie, listening to my dad's stories about our Czechoslovakian heritage. The magic to this recipe is the paprika with the sour cream. —JL

Lanelle Craig
Pleasant View, Tennessee

Ms. Georgie's Soup

Makes 12 servings

2 to 3 pounds ground chuck

3 (15-ounce) cans diced tomatoes, with liquid

1 (29-ounce) can tomato sauce

3 (15-ounce) cans black beans, drained and rinsed

2 (4-ounce) cans diced green chiles

2 to 3 (15-ounce) cans corn, with liquid

2 (1-ounce) packages original ranch dressing mix

1/2 cup diced red or green bell pepper

Brown the ground chuck in a large skillet over medium-high heat, about 15 minutes. Drain and mix with the remaining ingredients in a 6-quart slow cooker. Add extra water if desired to make the consistency you like. Cover and cook on low for 7 to 8 hours. ■

When my father was sick with cancer, my mother's neighbor would bring this soup over for the many visitors who would come to the house to help with him. It was warm and good, and everyone I have made it for since has wanted the recipe. —LC

soups & stews

Beefy Lentil Soup

Makes 6 to 8 servings

1 pound ground chuck

1 cup dried lentils, rinsed well

3 to 4 carrots, sliced 1/4 inch thick

3 to 4 stalks celery, chopped

1 medium onion, chopped

1/2 small head cabbage, chopped

1 medium green bell pepper, chopped

1 teaspoon salt

1/2 teaspoon black pepper

1/8 teaspoon cayenne

1 large bay leaf

2 beef bouillon cubes

1 (46-ounce) can tomato juice or tomato vegetable
     cocktail juice

1 quart water

Brown the ground chuck in a skillet over medium-high heat, 10 minutes. Drain and put in a 6-quart slow cooker with the remaining ingredients. Stir all the ingredients together gently to combine. Cover and cook on low for 8 to 10 hours, or on high for 4 to 5 hours. Serve in bowls. ■

Krista Rice
Highland Village, Texas

Ten-Can Soup

Makes 6 to 8 servings

2 pounds lean ground beef

2 (29-ounce) cans homestyle (larger cut) mixed vegetables

1 (15-ounce) can cut green beans

1 (15-ounce) can potatoes (precut or cut at home)

1 (15-ounce) can pinto beans

1 (15-ounce) can sweet corn

1 (10-ounce) can tomatoes with green chiles (we use mild)

2 (10-ounce) cans condensed minestrone soup

1 (15-ounce) can cut green beans with potatoes (optional)

Brown the ground beef in a large skillet over medium-high heat, about 12 minutes. Drain and transfer to a 6-quart slow cooker, then add the other ingredients with their liquids until full. Cover and cook on low for 7 to 8 hours. ∎

This soup is a family favorite and sooooo easy to make. We make it on the first really cold day of fall and the first day we have snow. When we come in from the cold, it really warms us up. —KR

soups & stews

Jerri Garofalo
Midlothian, Virginia

GiGi's
Italian Chicken Stew

Makes 8 servings

1 (3 1/2-pound) chicken

1 onion, quartered

2 carrots

3 stalks celery

4 whole cloves garlic, peeled

1 teaspoon salt

1/4 teaspoon dried basil

1 (28-ounce) can crushed or diced tomatoes, with liquid

1 (9-ounce) package fresh tortellini or small ravioli from
    refrigerator section of grocery store

Freshly grated Parmesan cheese, for serving (optional)

Rinse the chicken and remove as much skin as possible. Put the chicken in a 5-quart slow cooker and add the whole vegetables around the chicken. Then add about 2 cups of water. Season with salt and basil. Cover and cook on high for 2 to 3 hours or on low for 5 to 6 hours, until the chicken is done in the center or can be broken apart.

With a large slotted spoon or large tongs, remove the chicken from the broth and place in a large bowl or on a platter to cool. Remove the vegetables and allow to cool as well. While these are cooling, add the tomatoes and pasta to the broth in the slow cooker. Cover and cook on high until the pasta is almost done, about 30 minutes. Meanwhile, cut the vegetables into bite-sized pieces. Remove the meat from the bones and cut it into bite-sized pieces. Return the meat and vegetables to the cooker. Finish cooking until the pasta is al dente. Delicious dressed with Parmesan cheese. Serve with salad and crusty Italian bread. ■

This recipe came about when I needed to stretch a whole chicken for 8 people on a work night. To my good fortune it was delicious and like something from the old country. My husband's grandmother from Italy embraced me after dinner and told me it was just like she had taught me to cook. What a compliment! It is a wonderful dish to serve on a cold autumn or winter day. —JG

Sally Kelly
Akron, Ohio

Chicken Noodle Soup

Makes 4 to 6 servings

1 quart water

2 frozen skinless, boneless chicken breast halves

2 teaspoons instant chicken bouillon granules

1 tablespoon dehydrated minced onion

1 tablespoon dehydrated parsley flakes

3 carrots, chopped

2 stalks celery, chopped

1/4 teaspoon black pepper

1 teaspoon salt, or to taste (optional)

2 cups dried noodles or pasta of your choice, uncooked

Combine everything but the noodles in a 4-quart slow cooker. Cover and cook on low for 8 to 10 hours or on high for 4 to 5 hours. Cook the noodles in boiling water in a separate pot. Before serving, remove the chicken and shred with a fork; then add the chicken back to the slow cooker along with the cooked noodles. Cook long enough to heat the noodles if they have cooled.

If you like a starchier broth, add the uncooked noodles to the slow cooker when there is approximately 1 hour of cooking time left, until tender. ■

I am a huge soup fan! I came up with this recipe
one winter when I was searching for a chicken noodle
recipe to make in my slow cooker. All the recipes that I
had seen included ingredients that my family did not
particularly like. I needed something very basic—and this
is what I came up with. The broth is on the light side—
not too strongly chicken—but you can adjust that if you
wish. I hope you will enjoy it too! I love it because
I can throw it together in the morning and don't even have
to remember to thaw the chicken. Gotta love that! —SK

Sam Guinn
Gig Harbor, Washington

Chicken Tortilla Soup

Makes 6 servings

3 frozen skinless, boneless chicken breast halves
(about 1 pound)

1 (15-ounce) can diced tomatoes, with liquid

1 (10-ounce) can mild enchilada sauce

1 (4-ounce) can diced green chiles

1 (14-ounce) can chicken broth

1 (8-ounce) can corn, drained

1 teaspoon ground cumin

1 teaspoon salt

1/2 cup chopped onion

1 teaspoon chili powder

3 cloves garlic, minced, or 1 heaping tablespoon jarred
minced garlic

1 heaping tablespoon dried cilantro or a small handful of
fresh leaves

Tortilla chips, diced avocado, shredded cheddar cheese,
and sour cream, for serving

Put all the ingredients except the toppings into a 5-quart slow cooker and stir. Cover and cook on low for 6 to 7 hours or on high for 4 hours. Shred the chicken with two forks and dinner is ready! Serve with the toppings and enjoy! (Please follow these times and temperatures; otherwise the chicken will turn to mush.) ■

This recipe came to me from my best friend— she is quite the chef! I love it as my husband and kids are very picky eaters and they actually eat this! With how hectic it is to get out the door in the morning, it's so nice to just take 10 minutes and literally throw everything in the slow cooker and run. When we get home at night, dinner is on the table in 15 minutes. It's so delicious, and the toppings make it extra yummy! It's a great homemade, hot meal on a cold winter night. —SG

soups & stews

Laura Driscoll
Council Bluffs, Iowa

Laura's
Ham & Vegetable
Soup

Makes 6 to 8 servings

1 (3-pound) low-fat turkey ham, cut into 1-inch cubes

5 medium stalks celery, cut into 1-inch cubes

1/2 pound peeled carrots, cut into 1-inch pieces

1 medium onion, cut into 1-inch pieces

1 large sweet potato, peeled and cut into 1-inch cubes

1 medium rutabaga, peeled and cut into 1-inch cubes

1 large potato, peeled and cut into 1-inch cubes

1 (32-ounce) box low-fat chicken broth

16 to 32 ounces water (use the broth box)

1 teaspoon sea salt

1 teaspoon cracked black pepper

1 teaspoon minced fresh parsley

Put the ham and vegetables into a 6-quart slow cooker. Pour the broth and water over all and stir. Add the salt, pepper, and parsley, cover, and cook on low for 6 to 8 hours. ■

This soup is very easy to make and costs little. You can cut up the meat and vegetables the night before and keep, covered, in the refrigerator. —LD

Dolores Fernandez
Perris, California

Pozole
{Pork & Hominy Stew}

Makes 6 servings

1 1/2 pounds boneless pork, cut into 1-inch cubes

1 medium onion, diced

2 teaspoons minced garlic

2 (14-ounce) cans chicken broth

1 (14-ounce) can beef broth

1 (4-ounce) can diced green chiles

1 (10-ounce) can chile colorado or red enchilada sauce

3 (15-ounce) cans hominy, drained

Shredded cabbage and sliced radishes, for garnish

Lime wedges and tortillas, for serving

Put the pork, onion, garlic, chicken broth, beef broth, green chiles, and red sauce into a 5-quart slow cooker. Cover and cook on low for 6 to 7 hours or on high for 3 to 4 hours. Add the hominy. Let cook for another 15 minutes until heated through. Top each serving with shredded cabbage and sliced radishes. Serve with tortillas and a squeeze of lime. ∎

soups & stews

I like to make traditional Mexican recipes, but I want them to be fast and easy and still taste as good as the original recipe. —DF

Karen Waters
St. Louis Park, Minnesota

Southwestern
Black Bean Soup

Makes 4 to 6 servings

1 (12-ounce) bag dried black beans, sorted and rinsed

1 (4-ounce) can diced mild green chiles

1 teaspoon minced garlic

1 teaspoon dried cumin

1 teaspoon dried marjoram

1 teaspoon dried oregano

1/2 teaspoon ground cloves

1/4 teaspoon cayenne

2 quarts beef broth

1 medium onion, chopped

1 or 2 smoked ham hocks (about 1 1/2 pounds)

1 (6-ounce) can tomato paste

Sour cream, grated cheddar cheese, sliced green onions,
        and/or chopped fresh tomatoes, for serving

Soak the black beans overnight in water to cover and drain and rinse the next morning. Place all the ingredients into a 6-quart slow cooker, cover, and cook on high for 6 hours. Remove the ham hock after 6 hours to cool slightly. Remove the meat from the bones, chop it, and return it to the slow cooker until ready to serve. Top the soup with sour cream, grated cheddar cheese, green onions, and tomatoes as desired. Great with homemade corn bread and a tossed salad. ■

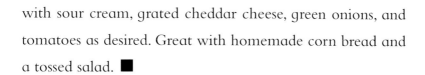

My family loves this hearty soup on a cold snowy night! The kids like the variety of toppings used to garnish the soup, and my husband loves the homemade corn bread that I bake to serve with this soup. —KW

soups&stews

Sharon Haschalk
Vassalboro, Maine

Mouthwatering
German Soup

Makes 4 to 6 servings

6 or 7 fresh bratwurst or Italian sausage links

1 small head cabbage, chopped

1 pound carrots, cut into 1-inch pieces

1 small turnip, cut into 1-inch pieces

1 medium onion, chopped

1 (28-ounce) can whole tomatoes, with liquid

2 bay leaves

2 teaspoons dried parsley flakes

1 teaspoon Worcestershire sauce

1 teaspoon Dijon mustard

2 teaspoons sugar

1 teaspoon garlic powder

1/4 teaspoon dried thyme leaves

1 to 2 teaspoons salt

1/2 teaspoon black pepper

3 cups water

1 (12-ounce) can beer

1 (3.5-ounce) package boil-in-bag rice, cooked
        and drained

Combine all the ingredients (start with 1 teaspoon of salt; you can always add another teaspoon if needed when the soup is done) except the beer and rice in a slow cooker. Cover and cook the soup on high for 3 to 4 hours or on low for 7 to 8 hours, until the vegetables are tender. Remove the sausage links during the last 30 minutes of cooking, cut into slices, return to the pot, and stir in the beer and cooked rice. Cook for a little longer until heated through. Serve with crusty bread of your choice. Enjoy! ■

My mother was German, and growing up she always made a lot of soup because it went a long way to feed eight children. There wasn't usually a lot of meat to go around, so in my recipe I have added more sausage than she would have been able to use. —SH

Andrea Hunt
Shorewood, Wisconsin

Minestrone

Makes 6 to 8 servings

1 large onion, finely chopped

3 cloves garlic, minced

2 tablespoons olive oil

1 pound Italian sausage (hot or mild or a mixture),
     casings peeled off

1 cup red wine

3 stalks celery, diced

3 carrots, diced

2 (14-ounce) cans chicken broth

1 cup water

1 (28-ounce) can diced tomatoes, with liquid

1 teaspoon Italian seasoning (basil, thyme, and oregano)

1 (15-ounce) can red kidney beans, with liquid

1 (15-ounce) can Great Northern beans, with liquid

Salt and black pepper

1 cup dried small pasta shells or other small shapes,
     uncooked

To make the soup, sauté the onion and garlic in the olive oil in a skillet over medium heat until softened, 4 to 5 minutes. Transfer to a 6-quart slow cooker. Add the sausage to the skillet and sauté until browned, 8 to 10 minutes. Transfer to the slow cooker. With the heat still on under the skillet, deglaze the pan with the wine, scraping up any browned bits of food, and boil the liquid until reduced by half. Pour the reduced wine into the slow cooker. Add the celery, carrots, broth, water, tomatoes, Itaian seasoning, beans, and salt and pepper to taste.

Cover and cook on low for 6 to 8 hours or on high for 3 to 4 hours. Add the pasta 20 minutes before serving and cook on high until al dente. ■

Yum! We serve this delicious soup-for-a-meal at every holiday party. You can vary the pasta and use seasonal shaped pastas. For vegetarian-style minestrone, switch to vegetable broth and leave out the sausage or substitute a meatless sausage. —AH

Julie Coles
Boise, Idaho

Meatball Stew

Makes 6 servings

1 1/2 pounds ground beef

2 teaspoons salt

1/8 teaspoon black pepper

1 egg

1 tablespoon minced onion

1/2 cup dry bread crumbs (I use Italian for added flavor)

1 tablespoon canola oil

3 tablespoons all-purpose flour

1 (15-ounce) can tomatoes, with liquid

1 teaspoon crushed dried basil

3 medium potatoes, peeled and diced

4 small carrots, peeled and diced

1 onion, coarsely chopped

1 stalk celery, sliced

Mix the beef, 1 1/2 teaspoons salt, pepper, egg, onion, and crumbs. Form into balls. Heat the oil in a large skillet on medium heat and brown the meatballs in batches. Drain on paper towels. Blend the flour into the fat in the skillet, then stir in the rest of the ingredients (including 1/2 teaspoon salt) and 1 cup water. Transfer to a 5-quart slow cooker. Add water to taste. Cover and cook on low for 8 hours. ■

Kathryn Marcuson
Elwood, Indiana

Garbanzo Bean
Soup

Makes 8 servings

1 (8-ounce) package sliced pepperoni

3 to 4 large potatoes, peeled and chopped

2 (15-ounce) cans garbanzo beans (chickpeas), drained

1 (15-ounce) can black beans, half of the liquid
    drained off (optional)

1/2 onion, chopped

1 teaspoon seasoned salt

2 dashes of black pepper

2 (48-ounce) cans chicken broth

Put all the ingredients into a 6-quart slow cooker. Turn it to low and cover it. Go away and leave it all day, 8 to 10 hours. Then come home to one terrific homemade meal. We like it with hot rolls, but the rest is up to you. ■

When we moved into our brand-new home in 1980, a dear teacher friend brought me a big pot of this soup. It was such a terrific comfort food, and it just couldn't get any simpler than this. Almost any of the ingredients can be adjusted to suit your family's tastes. Some people add tomatoes, but we like it without. —KM

Teresa Cheyney
Arco, Idaho

While You're Away
Stew

Makes 6 servings

2 pounds beef, lamb, or pork stew meat, cubed

3 medium carrots, sliced

2 onions, chopped

3 potatoes, peeled and quartered

About 1 cup leftover cooked vegetables (any kind) or
cooked or frozen peas

1 (10-ounce) can condensed tomato soup

1/2 can water, broth, or red wine (use the soup can)

Dash of black pepper

1 bay leaf

Put all the ingredients into a 6-quart slow cooker, mix, cover, and cook on high for 4 to 5 hours or on low for 7 to 8 hours. (This works well in the oven too: Combine the ingredients in a large casserole with a tight-fitting lid. Cover and bake at 275°F for 5 hours.) ■

I started making this when I worked part-time in the afternoons. It was so great to come home at the end of the day and smell that delicious stew. I usually put a pan of biscuits in the oven to bake while I prepared a salad, and then dinner was served! —TC

Marsha Konken
Sterling, Colorado

Vegetable Soup

Makes 4 to 6 servings

1 (15-ounce) can green beans, drained

1 (14-ounce) can whole kernel corn, drained

1 (8-ounce) can baby peas, drained

1 cup chopped celery, or to taste

1 cup chopped onion, or to taste

2 (14-ounce) cans beef broth

2 (10-ounce) cans condensed French onion soup

1 cup tomato juice

1 tablespoon Worcestershire sauce

2 beef bouillon cubes

Salt and black pepper

Combine the green beans, corn, peas, celery and onion to taste, the broth, onion soup, tomato juice, Worcestershire, bouillon cubes, and salt and pepper to taste in a 5-quart slow cooker and stir once. Cover and cook on low for 6 to 8 hours.

Serve with your favorite dinner rolls and a tossed salad. Makes a perfect wintertime supper. ■

soups & stews

Cindy Ulrich
Pittsburgh, Pennsylvania

JJ Soup

Makes 4 to 6 servings

1 1/2 pounds lean ground beef

2 tablespoons olive oil, if needed

Salt and black pepper

1 quart of your favorite spaghetti sauce

1 to 1 1/2 quarts water (use the sauce jar)

1/2 (16-ounce) bag baby carrots, preferably extra petite

1 to 2 (15-ounce) cans whole potatoes, or 4 medium
potatoes, peeled, cut into bite-sized pieces

1/2 (1-ounce) envelope onion soup mix

About 1 cup whole or cut frozen green beans (optional)

1/2 to 3/4 cup frozen yellow or white corn (optional)

Finely shredded sharp cheddar or cheddar/Monterey Jack
cheese, for serving (optional)

Brown the ground beef in a skillet over medium-high heat, 10 to 12 minutes, using olive oil if necessary to prevent sticking. Drain and rinse to remove the excess fat. Lightly season with salt and black pepper. Transfer the meat to a 6-quart slow cooker and add the spaghetti sauce, water,

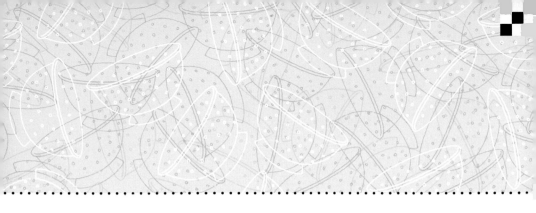

carrots, potatoes, and onion soup mix. Cover and cook on low all day.

About 10 minutes before serving, stir in the frozen green beans and corn, if using. (You could also heat them up separately and serve them on the side so people can add them to their own bowls if they want.) Ladle into soup bowls. Top with shredded cheese if desired. ■

This soup recipe was given to my mom over forty years ago, by a woman named "Jay." I'm not sure why we doubled the "J" but over the years we always have called it JJ Soup. It is a meal in itself, easy to let it cook all day, and served with crusty bread with butter and maybe some cottage cheese. There's nothing better than coming into the house to the scent permeating the room and knowing we're having JJ Soup for dinner! —CU

soups & stews

All cooking is
a matter of time.
In general, the more time
the better.

—John Erskine

Beef Dishes

Allison Kanagy
Arlington, Texas

Nanaw's
Sunday Roast

Makes 6 to 8 servings

1 (3- to 4-pound) boneless beef chuck roast,
   trimmed of excess fat

3 tablespoons Greek seasoning

1/2 teaspoon cayenne

1 1/2 teaspoons kosher salt

1 tablespoon freshly ground black pepper

3 tablespoons olive oil

1 (15-ounce) can crushed tomatoes, with liquid

1 quart water

1 (10-ounce) can chicken broth

1 (12-ounce) can cola

1 cup dark roux (either homemade or from a jar)

1 sprig fresh rosemary

4 sprigs fresh thyme

2 bay leaves

2 tablespoons tomato paste

3 yellow onions, quartered

2 teaspoons garlic puree or 1 tablespoon crushed
   fresh garlic

6 to 8 medium carrots, peeled and halved crosswise

4 potatoes, peeled and quartered

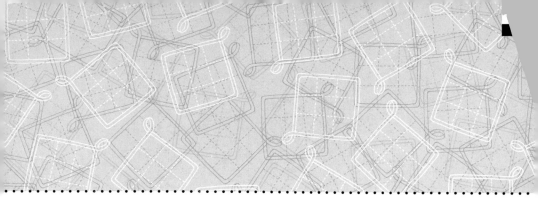

2 stalks celery, chopped into 1-inch pieces

1 cup button mushrooms, stemmed and halved (optional)

3 tablespoons finely chopped fresh parsley

Season all sides of the beef with the Greek seasoning, cayenne, salt, and black pepper. In a large Dutch oven or other heavy pot, heat the oil over medium-high heat. Brown the meat on all sides, taking the time to get a nice crust on the outside, 12 to 15 minutes. Remove the roast and place in a 7-quart slow cooker.

In the still-hot pan used to brown the roast, combine the tomatoes, water, broth, and cola. Bring to a simmer. Stir in the roux. Add the rosemary, thyme, bay leaves, and tomato paste. Bring to a boil and cook for 5 minutes. Carefully pour into the slow cooker. Cover and cook on high for 3 hours.

Scatter the vegetables around the pot roast. Add more water if needed. Cover the slow cooker and reduce the heat to low. Cook for 4 to 6 hours, until the beef and

{continued}

beef dishes

vegetables are fork-tender. Remove the rosemary twig and the bay leaves. Add the parsley. Remove the pot roast and arrange on a platter surrounded by the vegetables. We serve this with steamed rice because the gravy is SO good! Leftovers are great chopped up and served po'boy style! ■

My Nanaw (my maternal grandmother, whom I loved more than anything!) used to make this. She was a marvelous cook and everyone loved to be invited for one of her meals. She was also a wonderfully funny and well-loved hostess. This roast is easy, flavorful, and always a hit with family and friends! The roux gives the gravy body and "soul" that when combined with the seasoning is delicious! Mushrooms were optional because my siblings did not like them. Nanaw always removed the stems and used them for other things because she said they got a bit "slick" in the slow cooker (as they say in East Texas!). —AX

Shelly Moquin
Lynnwood, Washington

Holiday Pot Roast

Makes 6 servings

1 (3-pound) beef rump roast, trimmed of fat

Vegetable oil cooking spray

1 (15-ounce) can whole-berry cranberry sauce

2 cups vegetable broth

1 teaspoon cracked black pepper

2 teaspoons Trader Joe's 21 Seasoning Salute

2 fresh bay leaves

3 fresh sage leaves

1/2 cup finely chopped fresh parsley

2 Walla Walla sweet onions, thinly sliced

1 1/2 pounds baby carrots

Place the roast in a Dutch oven sprayed with cooking spray and brown on both sides, 12 to 15 minutes.

In a bowl, mix the cranberry sauce, vegetable broth, pepper, seasoning blend, bay leaves, sage, and parsley. Put into a 6-quart slow cooker. Place the roast in the slow cooker. Add the onions. Cover and cook on low for 4 hours, add the carrots, and cook for another 4 hours. Voilà! Add a salad and some rolls and you have dinner at 6:00 P.M.! ∎

beef dishes

67

Cheryl Culver
Perkins, Oklahoma

Easy Gravy
Pot Roast

Makes 6 servings

1 (3- to 4-pound) boneless beef chuck roast

1 1/2 teaspoons seasoned salt (or saltless seasoning)

1/4 cup vegetable oil

1 medium onion, thinly sliced

3 bay leaves

3 or 4 beef bouillon cubes, crushed

4 cloves garlic, pressed

1 (10-ounce) can condensed cream of mushroom soup

1/2 cup white wine

1/2 pound baby carrots

2 cups sliced mushrooms

Rub the roast on all sides with the seasoning salt. In a skillet, heat the oil over high heat and sear the roast until browned all over, 12 to 15 minutes. Place the roast in a 5-quart slow cooker and add the onion, bay leaves, bouillon cubes, garlic, and soup. Add the white wine, 1 cup of water, and the carrots and mushrooms. Cover and cook on low for 6 to 9 hours. Turn off the slow cooker and let it rest for about 15 minutes before serving. This makes a nice creamy gravy that is very flavorful. ■

Ruth Lloyd
Murfreesboro, Tennessee

Mom's Pot Roast
& Gravy

Makes 4 to 6 servings

1 large (3- to 4-pound) rump or arm beef pot roast

2 tablespoons seasoned salt (such as Lawry's)

Black pepper

1 medium onion, chopped

4 small potatoes, peeled and chopped

3 large carrots, chopped

2 (14-ounce) cans beef broth

1/2 cup milk

3 tablespoons all-purpose flour

Place the roast in a 6-quart slow cooker and season with 1 tablespoon of the seasoned salt and some pepper. Place the onion, potatoes, and carrots on top of the roast and pour the beef broth over all. Sprinkle the remaining tablespoon of seasoned salt over the top. Cover and cook on low for 6 to 9 hours (more or less, depending on how your slow cooker cooks). After the roast is done, spoon out the liquid into a small saucepan. Whisk the milk and flour together in a small bowl. Slowly add to the saucepan and stir until the gravy thickens. ∎

beef dishes

Char Pletcher
Lone Grove, Oklahoma

Char's Roast

Makes 6 to 8 servings

1 (4- to 5-pound) boneless beef arm or chuck roast

4 medium white potatoes, peeled and cubed

4 medium carrots, sliced

1 medium onion, chopped (optional)

2 stalks celery (optional)

1 (1-ounce) envelope dry onion soup mix

1 (1-ounce) package beef gravy mix

1 (1-ounce) package ranch dressing mix

Place the roast in a 6-quart slow cooker. Add the vegetables. Blend together the mixes and 1 cup of water, then pour over the meat. Cover and set to low. Cook for 8 to 10 hours. Using a slow cooker bag is a plus! ∎

This is the best-flavored roast, and there's no need to season other than the dry mixes. I add the onion because it's more visible than the dried onion in the mix. My family just loves this, and it's so good, especially on a cold night. The smell when you walk in the door is heavenly! —CP

Michelle Purdy
Pine City, Minnesota

Tender Roast Beef

Makes 4 to 6 servings

4 carrots, quartered

5 potatoes, peeled and quartered

1 (3- to 4-pound) boneless beef chuck roast

1 medium onion, sliced

4 cloves garlic, minced

1 (12-ounce) can beer

Salt and black pepper

Put the carrots and potatoes in the bottom of a slow cooker. Add the trimmed meat, onion, and garlic. Pour in the beer and add some salt and pepper. Set the slow cooker on low, cover, and cook for 6 to 9 hours. ■

This is a hearty, simple, stick-to-your-ribs kind of meal. It also makes a wonderful beef stew with the leftovers. The next day, put all the leftovers in the slow cooker, including the liquid. Add a large can of cream of mushroom soup, 2 cups of chopped green cabbage, and 1 drained 15-ounce can of peas. Cook until the cabbage is soft. —MP

beef dishes

71

Allison Kanagy
Arlington, Texas

Brisket Bye Bye

Makes 8 to 10 servings

2 tablespoons ancho chile powder

2 tablespoons salt

1 tablespoon garlic powder

1 tablespoon onion powder

2 tablespoons black pepper

1 tablespoon sugar

2 teaspoons dry mustard

1 bay leaf, crushed

1 tablespoon dried thyme

2 tablespoons Greek seasoning

1 (4-pound) beef brisket, trimmed and cut into a few pieces
      to fit into the slow cooker, if necessary

2 cups beef broth

1 (12-ounce) can beer or cola, at room temperature

1/2 cup apple juice, at room temperature

1/4 cup pineapple juice, at room temperature

1/4 cup Worcestershire sauce

1 tablespoon soy sauce

2 tablespoons chopped canned chipotle chiles in adobo

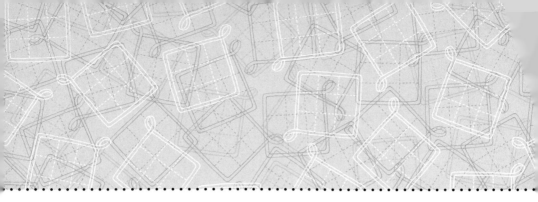

Combine the chile powder, salt, garlic powder, onion powder, pepper, sugar, mustard, bay leaf, thyme, and Greek seasoning and rub over the brisket. Place in a 5-quart slow cooker, cover, and cook on high for 2 hours. Turn over and cook for another 2 hours. Add the broth, beer, juices, Worcestershire, soy sauce, and chiles. Cover and cook on low for 3 to 5 hours, or until tender. It needs to maintain a 300°F temperature. Some slow cookers may need to be turned up to high. Trim the fat and slice the meat thinly across the grain. Top with juice from the pan. ∎

Brisket is inexpensive and easy to prepare in the slow cooker. This always satisfies our hungriest. We serve it with macaroni and cheese and salad. Top the meal off with cobbler and you can't beat the smiles! —AK

Stephani Nelson
Olympia, Washington

The Best
Barbecue Beef!

Makes 10 to 12 servings

1 cup sliced onion

1 tablespoon butter

1 (3 1/2-pound) boneless beef chuck roast

1 1/2 cups ketchup

1/4 cup firmly packed brown sugar

1/4 cup red wine vinegar

2 tablespoons Dijon mustard

2 tablespoons Worcestershire sauce

1 teaspoon liquid smoke

1/2 teaspoon garlic salt

10 to 12 sandwich buns

In a saucepan over medium heat, stir the onion and butter together until nicely browned, about 15 minutes. Place the chuck roast in a 6-quart slow cooker. Combine the ketchup, brown sugar, vinegar, mustard, Worcestershire, liquid smoke, and garlic salt in a large bowl. Stir in the caramelized onions. Pour the barbecue sauce mixture over the chuck roast. Cover and cook on low for 6 to 9 hours or on high for 3 to 4 hours. Remove the chuck roast from the slow cooker when very tender and shred the meat with a fork. Place the shredded meat back in the slow cooker and stir to coat

evenly with the sauce. Spoon the meat onto sandwich buns and top with the remaining barbecue sauce if desired. ■

This recipe is one of my family's favorites. I came up with it when we were in the middle of moving and I needed something to feed everyone who was helping with the move. I knew how to make barbecue sauce, and I thought, Why not try it with the meat in a slow cooker? Through the years I have adjusted this recipe—I'm always adding some new ingredient to it! —SM

beef dishes

Cheryle Switzer
The Colony, Texas

BBQ Boneless
Short Ribs

Makes 4 servings

1 1/2 pounds boneless beef short ribs

2 green bell peppers, cut into large chunks

1 large onion, cut into large chunks

5 stalks celery, cut into large chunks

1 (8-ounce) package fresh mushrooms,
     cut into large chunks

1 1/2 cups honey barbecue sauce

Put the short ribs on the bottom of a 5-quart slow cooker. Add the green peppers, onion, celery, and mushrooms. Pour the barbecue sauce over all. Cover and cook on low for 6 to 8 hours. ∎

This is an easy recipe I could start in the morning as I was getting the children ready for school. Would be ready for supper after homework. It really smells good when you open the door, too! —CS

76

Ann Rice

Monrovia, California

BBQ Beef
Sandwiches

Makes 6 servings

1 1/2 pounds lean boneless beef arm chuck roast

1/4 cup ketchup

1 tablespoon brown sugar

1 tablespoon red wine vinegar

1 1/2 teaspoons Dijon mustard

1 1/2 teaspoons Worcestershire sauce

1 clove garlic, crushed

1/4 teaspoon salt

1/4 teaspoon liquid smoke

1/8 teaspoon black pepper

6 French rolls or sandwich buns

Place the beef in a 3-quart slow cooker. Combine the remaining ingredients except the rolls in a bowl; pour over the meat. Cover and cook on low for 6 to 8 hours. Remove the beef from the slow cooker and shred with two forks. Combine the beef with 1/2 cup of the sauce from the slow cooker. Spoon the meat and sauce mixture onto warmed rolls. Top with additional sauce if desired. ■

beef dishes

Christine Geery
Salt Lake City, Utah

Short Ribs
in Beer

Makes 4 to 5 servings

1/4 cup all-purpose flour

1 teaspoon dry mustard

1/2 teaspoon paprika

1 teaspoon salt

1/4 teaspoon black pepper

4 pounds beef bone-in short ribs, wiped dry

2 tablespoons oil

1 large onion, sliced

1 to 2 tablespoons molasses, to taste

1/4 cup ketchup

3 tablespoons cider vinegar

1 (12-ounce) can beer

1/2 teaspoon hot sauce (optional)

Mix together the flour, dry mustard, paprika, salt, and pepper and dredge the ribs in the mixture, reserving the excess flour mixture. Heat the oil in a large skillet and brown the ribs on all sides, 10 to 15 minutes. Transfer the ribs to a 6-quart slow cooker. Dredge the onion in the rest of the flour and sauté in the skillet over medium heat until tender, 5 to 10 minutes. Transfer the onion and any browned bits to the slow

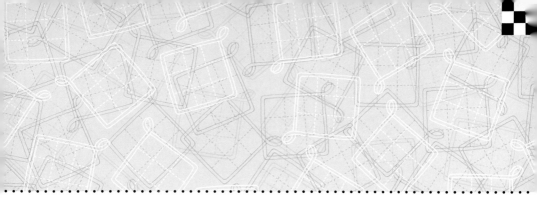

cooker. Stir together the molasses, ketchup, vinegar, beer, and hot sauce. Pour all over the ribs and onion. Cover and cook on low for 7 to 8 hours or on high for 3 to 4 hours, depending on your slow cooker. Serve with lots of cooked rice and veggies of your choice. ■

This is a wonderful cold-weather meal that my family has loved for years. The sauce is so delicious you may want to double it. The aroma itself will send so many waves of pleasure through your senses that you just may decide that it will be a meal for all seasons. —CG

beef dishes

Pam Sumner
Mesa, Arizona

Sloppy Joes

Makes 8 to 10 servings

2 pounds lean ground beef

2 onions, chopped

6 stalks celery, chopped

1 (6-ounce) can tomato paste

1 (8-ounce) can tomato sauce

1 cup barbecue sauce (or diced tomatoes and
    green chiles for a little more zip)

1 teaspoon salt

1 teaspoon black pepper

1 tablespoon sugar

1 tablespoon vinegar

Brown the ground beef with the onions and celery in a large skillet over medium-high heat and drain, 12 to 15 minutes. Combine all the ingredients in a 4-quart slow cooker. Cover and cook on low for 3 to 4 hours or until ready to eat. ∎

I like to have this when hosting a water volleyball party so no one has to opt out of the games to barbecue. Have the guests bring a dish to share and you're good to go. —PS

Jane Hull
Long Beach, California

Salsa Star Supper

Makes 4 to 6 servings

1 (1-pound) beef flank steak or London broil

1 cup salsa of your choice

Flour or corn tortillas, warmed, for serving

Shredded cheese, chopped tomato, shredded lettuce,
    chopped onion, guacamole or cubed
    avocado, chopped cilantro, or your other favorite
    taco toppings, for serving

Place the meat in a 3-quart slow cooker. Pour the salsa over it. Turn the cooker to low, cover, and forget it for 6 to 7 hours. To serve, separate the beef into strands (like pulled pork) and serve in warm flour or corn tortillas with your favorite taco toppings. Or cut into chunks (careful, it is fall-apart-tender) and place on top of a scoop of mashed potatoes or rice and drizzle a little of the sauce over. ■

My sister-in-law, Donna, gave me this idea. She keeps two slow cookers and uses one for the meal and one for the side. She is awesome, running her business and taking care of family. The salsa can be mild, medium, hot, roasted pepper, peach, mango, or whatever tickles your fancy! It will always turn out delicious! The star part is you! —JH

beef dishes

Kathy Lowe
Orem, Utah

Shredded Beef Tacos

Makes 10 to 12 servings

4 to 5 pounds boneless beef chuck roast

1/2 red onion, chopped

3 cloves garlic, peeled

1/4 cup oil

1 to 3 teaspoons hot red pepper flakes

2 teaspoons ground cumin

2 teaspoons dried oregano

1 teaspoon black pepper

10 to 12 (10-inch) flour tortillas, warmed

Shredded lettuce, chopped onion, chopped tomato,
        sour cream, and salsa, for serving

Pour 1 cup of water into a 6-quart slow cooker, add the roast, and set aside. Combine the onion, garlic, oil, red pepper flakes, cumin, oregano, and pepper in a blender. Blend and pour over the roast. Cover and cook on low for 7 to 9 hours, until the roast is very tender. Shred the roast with two forks and return the meat to the slow cooker. Cover and cook on low for 1 hour. Fill the tortillas with the beef mixture and add toppings as desired. ∎

Lorraine Tyler
Richwood, Texas

Taco Casserole

Makes 6 servings

1 pound ground round

1/2 cup chopped bell pepper

1/2 cup chopped onion

1 teaspoon salt-free garlic and herb seasoning, or to taste

1 (10-ounce) can condensed lower-fat/sodium cream of
   mushroom soup

1 (10-ounce) can condensed lower-fat/sodium cream of
   chicken soup

1 (10-ounce) can condensed cheddar cheese soup

1 (10-ounce) can diced tomatoes with green chiles,
   regular or mild

1 (12-ounce) bag nacho-flavored tortilla chips

2 cups grated cheddar or Colby-Jack cheese

Cook the ground round with the bell pepper and onion in a skillet over medium heat until the meat is browned, 8 to 10 minutes. Season with the garlic and herb seasoning. Combine the soups and tomatoes in a large bowl, add the meat mixture, and mix well. Crush the tortilla chips in the bag into small pieces and add to the mixture. Mix well and pour into a 4-quart slow cooker. Top with the cheese, cover, and cook on low for 3 to 4 hours. ■

beef dishes

Theresa Norsky
Cohocton, New York

Granny's
German Goulash

Makes 6 to 8 servings

1 pound beef stew meat, cut into cubes

1 pound boneless pork, cut into cubes

3 large onions, cut into half rings or chunks—enough to
    equal the amount of meat

2 tablespoons vegetable shortening

1 tablespoon paprika

1 tablespoon caraway seeds

1 teaspoon salt

1 teaspoon black pepper

1/2 teaspoon cayenne

1 large beef bouillon cube

3 tablespoons all-purpose flour

1 cup sour cream

2 cups water or 1 (12-ounce) bottle beer

Flat egg noodles or spaetzle (homemade or boxed)

Butter and minced parsley for the noodles

Cook the beef, pork, and onions in the shortening in
a large skillet over medium-high heat until very brown,
10 to 12 minutes. Add the paprika, caraway, salt, black
pepper, cayenne, and bouillon cube. Sprinkle the flour onto

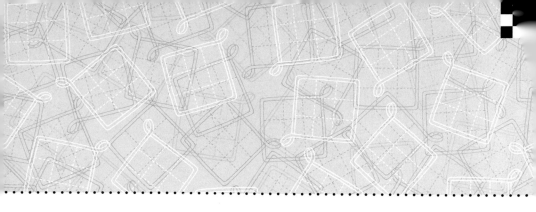

this mixture and stir until fully incorporated (like a roux). Transfer all of this to a 4-quart slow cooker. Add the water. Cover and cook on low for 6 to 8 hours, untilthe meat is very tender. Stir in the sour cream about 10 minutes before serving. Boil the noodles or spaetzle, butter liberally, and sprinkle with parsley. Transfer to a bowl and top with the goulash. Goes very well with beer or milk. ■

Opa grew up in Germany, and Papa grew up in Poland. Both claim their country is where goulash comes from (no one dares to tell them it's actually from Hungary!). But this is one of those stick-to-your-ribs meals that is so wonderful on a cool fall day or a frosty winter day. It ages well if you actually have leftovers; the following day or two the flavors marry and become very rich. And both Opa and Papa are absolute teddy bears after filling up on this great stew. —JN

Rebecca Langford
Gridley, California

Lasagna

Makes 6 to 8 servings

2 links Italian sausage, casings removed

1/2 pound ground beef

1/2 white onion, chopped

2 (26-ounce) jars any pasta sauce

1 (15-ounce) container ricotta cheese

1 (8-ounce) package grated Italian blend cheese

1/2 (1-pound) box lasagna noodles, broken into pieces

Brown the meat in a large skillet over medium-high heat, chopping it into pieces, 8 to 10 minutes. Add the onion and cook to soften, then drain. Spray a 6-quart slow cooker with nonstick spray. Pour 1/2 jar of sauce into the bottom of the slow cooker. Layer the meat, ricotta, Italian blend cheese, noodles, and all but 1/4 cup of the remaining sauce in the slow cooker until all the ingredients are used up. Pour the remaining 1/4 cup sauce on top, cover, and cook on low for 4 to 5 hours. This can be made with different types of ground meat. To make it meatless, just add more noodles and cheese. ■

Janet Corcoran
Davenport, Iowa

Sweet–Sour
Beef & Vegetables

Makes 8 servings

2 pounds beef round or chuck steak, cubed

2 tablespoons oil

2 (8-ounce) cans tomato sauce

2 teaspoons chili powder

2 teaspoons paprika

2 tablespoons sugar

1 teaspoon salt

1/2 cup cider vinegar

1/2 cup light Karo syrup

2 cups carrots in 1/4-inch-thick slices

2 cups small white onions, peeled, or 1 (15-ounce) can or
      jar of onions, drained

2 large green bell peppers, cut into 1-inch squares

Cooked rice, noodles, or macaroni, for serving

Brown the meat in the oil in a large skillet over medium-high heat, 10 to 12 minutes; transfer to a 6-quart slow cooker. Add the remaining ingredients and mix well. Cover and cook on low for 6 to 7 hours or on high for 3 to 4 hours. Serve over rice, noodles, or macaroni. ■

beef dishes

Nancy Wethington
St. Louis, Missouri

American-Style
Boeuf Bourguignon

Makes 6 servings

3 pounds lean beef stew meat, cubed

All-purpose flour, for dredging

1 tablespoon olive oil

1 large onion, cut in half and thinly sliced

1 clove garlic, chopped, or to taste

1/4 cup dry red wine

2 teaspoons L. B. Jamison's beef-flavored soup base,
    melted in 1 cup hot water

1 cup baby carrots (optional)

Prepared Betty Crocker instant garlic mashed potatoes,
    for serving

Dredge the meat in flour to coat. Heat a large nonstick skillet, add the olive oil, and then brown the meat cubes in batches, without crowding them, 12 to 15 minutes. Set a 5-quart slow cooker to low to preheat it while you brown the meat. Transfer the meat as it browns to the slow cooker. Add the onion and garlic to the skillet and brown lightly, 4 to 5 minutes. Add the wine and scrape up any pan drippings. Add to the slow cooker. Add the beef broth, cover, and cook on low for 7 to 8 hours. For each

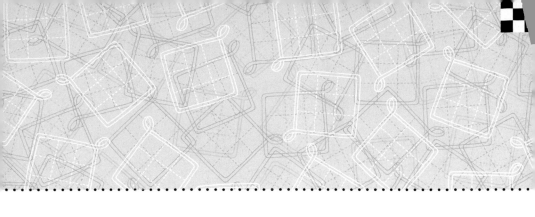

serving, put a dollop (or two) of garlic mashed potatoes on the plate and then ladle the Beef Bourguignon to the side and on top of the potatoes. Serve piping hot! ■

This is the easiest way to have a deliciously rich, flavorful meal. The instant mashed potatoes are the perfect accompaniment. And it's especially easy for midweek dinner guests: comforting, homey, and tastes like you slaved for hours over the stove! Put on an apron, slap some flour on your face, and no one will know the truth behind this recipe! —NW

beef dishes

Pam Sumner
Mesa, Arizona

Inexpensive
Beef Stroganoff

Makes 6 to 8 servings

2 pounds beef stew meat, cut into 1-inch pieces

1 onion, thinly sliced

1 (10-ounce) can condensed cream of mushroom soup

1 (2-ounce) package onion soup mix

1 (4-ounce) can mushroom pieces, drained

1 cup dry red wine or red cooking wine

1 teaspoon salt

1 teaspoon black pepper

1 cup sour cream

1 (10-ounce) package egg noodles

Put the meat, onion, cream of mushroom soup, onion soup mix, mushroom pieces, red wine, salt, and black pepper into a 4-quart slow cooker, cover, and cook on low for 6 hours. Stir in the sour cream (or leave it out and serve it on the side at the table). Boil and drain the noodles. Serve the stroganoff over the noodles. ■

This is delicious and so easy to put together.
Add a tossed salad and some hot rolls to make
a wonderful comfort food dinner. —PS

Ann Mueller
Olympia, Washington

Stew Meat
& Noodles

Makes 4 servings

1 pound beef stew meat, trimmed

1 (10-ounce) can condensed tomato soup

1 (10-ounce) can condensed cream of mushroom soup

1/2 cup red wine

8 to 10 ounces egg noodles

Cook the stew meat in the microwave till partially cooked and drain well. Put the meat in a 4-quart slow cooker, add the soups, and stir. Cover and cook on low for 4 to 5 hours. About an hour before eating, add the red wine. Cook the egg noodles and drain well. Add them to the stew or divide them among the plates and serve the stew on top. ∎

This recipe can be increased for more people. You can add more soup or substitute cream of celery or your choice. Cook more egg noodles for a larger crowd. When the kids were home, they all liked this— sometimes we ran out! It's an easy meal for a busy family and can be reheated. —AM

beef dishes

Sandy Preister
Papillion, Nebraska

Beef Tips

Makes 4 to 6 servings

2 pounds beef round steak, cubed

1 (1-ounce) package dry brown gravy mix

1 (10-ounce) can condensed cream of mushroom soup with
roasted garlic

1/2 cup water

1 tablespoon Worcestershire sauce

1/2 teaspoon seasoned salt

Dash of black pepper

2 or 3 beef bouillon cubes

Mashed potatoes or cooked egg noodles, for serving

Brown the beef lightly in a skillet over medium heat, 10 to 12 minutes. You may want to spray the pan with nonstick cooking spray if necessary to prevent sticking. Mix the gravy mix, soup, water, Worcestershire, seasoned salt, and pepper together. Put the meat into a 3-quart slow cooker, pour the gravy mixture on top, and stir to combine. Drop in the bouillon cubes, cover, and cook on low for 6 to 7 hours. Serve over mashed potatoes or noodles. ■

Mary Monahan
Tualatin, Oregon

Porcupine Meatballs

Makes 6 servings

2 pounds ground beef

1 1/2 cups instant rice, uncooked

1/2 cup chopped onion

2 eggs

1/2 cup grated cheddar cheese

1 teaspoon salt

Black pepper

About 1 cup all-purpose flour

About 1/2 cup oil

1 (10-ounce) can condensed tomato soup

1 (8-ounce) can tomato sauce

1/2 cup water

Combine the ground beef, rice, onion, eggs, cheese, salt, and pepper to taste in a large bowl; mix well. Shape into 1-inch balls. Roll in flour. Heat the oil in a skillet and brown the meatballs all over in batches, if necessary. (The meatballs will continue to cook in the slow cooker.) Place the meatballs in a 5-quart slow cooker. Mix the soup, tomato sauce, and water in a bowl. Pour over the meatballs, cover, and cook on low for 4 hours. ∎

beef dishes

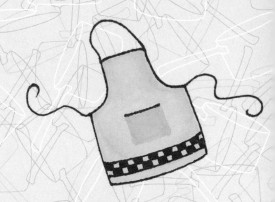

Learn how to cook—
try new recipes,
learn from your mistakes,
be fearless,
and above all have fun!

—Julia Child

Poultry Dishes

Marcie Phillips
Lebanon, Oregon

Marcie's Chicken

Makes 6 servings

2 to 3 pounds chicken thighs (12 to 15), skinned

2 cups water

2/3 cup soy sauce

2/3 cup cider vinegar

2 to 3 heaping teaspoons pickling spice

Cooked rice, for serving

Place the chicken, water, soy sauce, and vinegar in a 4-quart slow cooker. Either tie the pickling spice in a piece of cheesecloth or put it in two metal tea balls. Toss it in, turn the slow cooker to low, cover, and cook for 7 to 9 hours. When the chicken falls apart, take it out, pick all the chicken off the bones, and throw the meat back into the slow cooker. Remove and discard the pickling spice. Serve the chicken over rice. ∎

My parents lived in Alaska for a long time, and this was something my mother started making while there. I think the fishing boats served a version of it while out to sea. The longer you cook it, the yummier it gets. —MP

Mary Monahan
Tualatin, Oregon

MaryAnn's Chicken

Makes 6 servings

4 to 6 skinless, boneless chicken breasts

1 (16-ounce) jar sun-dried tomato Alfredo sauce

2 (4-ounce) cans portobello mushrooms, drained

1 (8-ounce) package cream cheese

Cooked egg noodles or rice, for serving

Place the chicken in a 4-quart slow cooker. Combine the sauce and mushrooms and pour over the top. Cover and cook on low for 5 to 7 hours. Cube the cream cheese and add it to the slow cooker in the last hour of cooking. Stir well. Serve over hot noodles or rice. ∎

A gift from my stepmother, who is often sharing delicious recipes from her kitchen. —MM

poultry dishes

Rebecca Baker
Martinsville, Indiana

Chicken & Vegetables

Makes 4 to 6 servings

2 (10-ounce) cans condensed cream of chicken soup

1 pound skinless, boneless chicken breasts

4 carrots, cut into 1-inch pieces

4 potatoes, peeled and cut into 1-inch pieces

1 large onion, cut into 1-inch pieces

2 stalks celery, cut into 1-inch pieces

2 teaspoons salt

1 teaspoon black pepper

2 tablespoons butter

Put 1/2 can of the soup in the bottom of a slow cooker. Layer half of the chicken, carrots, potatoes, onion, and celery with 1 teaspoon salt and 1/2 teaspoon black pepper on top. Pour 1 can of the remaining soup over those ingredients. Layer the rest of the ingredients in the same way, ending with 1/2 can of soup on top. Dot with the butter. Cover and cook on low for 6 to 8 hours or on high for 3 to 4 hours. ■

My family loves this recipe! It makes its own gravy. I just make a quick salad and dinner is served! —RB

Jan Thomason
Center Point, Texas

Thomason Ranch Amazing
Chicken-in-a-Pot

Makes 4 to 6 servings

Vegetable oil spray

6 large red potatoes, quartered

Salt and black pepper

1 (16-ounce) package baby carrots

1 (3- to 4-pound) whole chicken, rinsed inside and out,
   any gizzards removed

Seasoning of your choice

1 (10-ounce) can condensed cream of chicken soup

Spray the inside of a 6-quart slow cooker with nonstick spray. Add the potatoes and salt and pepper. Add the carrots, spreading them out on top of the potatoes. Salt and pepper your chicken after patting it dry and lay it on top of the carrots. You can use a favorite seasoning—my favorite is a garlic/pepper mix. Spread the soup over the chicken. Cover and cook 7 to 9 hours on low. ■

Easy peasy lemon squeezy! . . .
and AMAZING! —JT

poultry dishes

99

Jeannie Stack
Longwood, Florida

Hawaiian Chicken

Makes 4 to 6 servings

1 (3- to 4-pound) whole chicken, rinsed and cut into 8 pieces

Salt and black pepper

1 large onion, cut into 1-inch pieces

1 green bell pepper, cut into 1-inch pieces

1 (8-ounce or 20-ounce) can pineapple chunks in juices,
     with liquid

1 tablespoon prepared minced garlic or 2 cloves garlic,
     minced

1/2 cup brown sugar, dipped and leveled off, not packed

Cooked rice, for serving

Season the chicken with salt and pepper. Put the onion and green pepper into the bottom of a 6-quart slow cooker. Place the chicken on top of the vegetables and then pour the pineapple chunks on top of the chicken. Sprinkle the garlic and brown sugar on top. Cover and cook on low for 7 to 9 hours or until the chicken reaches 170°F on an instant-read thermometer. Serve over rice. ■

This was one of my children's fave recipes. You can also make this on top of the stove in a skillet. Just cover it and simmer for a couple of hours. Yummy! —JS

Merrill Hogan-Smith
Yallambie, Victoria, Australia

Cacciatore Chicken

Makes 4 to 6 servings

Vegetable oil cooking spray

2 onions, sliced

2 to 3 pounds skinless, boneless chicken breasts or thighs

2 (6-ounce) cans tomato paste

1 (4-ounce) can sliced mushrooms, drained

2 teaspoons minced garlic

1 teaspoon dried basil

1 teaspoon dried oregano

1 cup dry white wine

Spray the inside of a 4-quart slow cooker with oil. Put the sliced onions in the slow cooker Cut the chicken into pieces and place in the cooker. In a bowl, mix the tomato paste, mushrooms, garlic, basil, oregano, and wine and pour over the chicken. Cover and cook on low for 5 to 7 hours or on high for 3 hours. ■

This recipe is supereasy and superyummy! Sometimes I add other veggies such as peppers, zucchini, peas, or celery. We like to eat it with rice or mashed potatoes, but you can please yourself. I hope you enjoy it. —MH-S

poultry dishes

Kara Enos
Fresno, California

Chicken Cacciatore
with Mashed Potatoes

Makes 4 to 6 servings

Chicken Cacciatore

1 (3- to 4-pound) whole chicken, rinsed and patted dry

1 cup shredded carrots

1 medium yellow bell pepper, cut into bite-sized pieces

1 medium green bell pepper, cut into bite-sized pieces

1 medium onion, chopped

2 (28-ounce) cans San Marzano peeled tomatoes,
    with liquid

1 cup low-sodium chicken broth

1 teaspoon sea salt

1/2 teaspoon freshly ground black pepper

3 cloves garlic, chopped

2 teaspoons chopped fresh flat-leaf parsley

1/2 teaspoon dried rosemary, crushed

1 teaspoon dried oregano, crushed

12 fresh basil leaves, sliced or chopped

Mashed Potatoes

12 medium russet potatoes, peeled and cut into
    1-inch cubes

2 teaspoons sea salt

8 tablespoons (1 stick) butter (not margarine)

1 teaspoon iodized salt

1 teaspoon black pepper

1/2 teaspoon garlic powder

1/2 to 3/4 cup evaporated milk

To make the chicken cacciatore, place the chicken in a 6-quart slow cooker. Add the carrots, bell peppers, and onion. In a separate large bowl, mix the canned tomatoes, chicken broth, sea salt, black pepper, garlic, parsley, rosemary, oregano, and basil. Pour the mixture over the chicken and vegetables. Cover and cook on high for 4 hours, then turn the heat to low and cook for another 4 hours. The chicken will be falling-off-the-bone tender. Serve over the mashed potatoes with the sauce.

To make the mashed potatoes, put the potatoes into an 8-quart pot. Fill with water until the potatoes are covered. Add the sea salt. Bring to a boil over high heat. Then turn the heat down to medium-high and simmer for 20 minutes, until the potatoes are fork-tender but not falling

{continued}

poultry dishes

Chicken Cacciatore
with Mashed Potatoes {continued}

apart. Drain out all the water. Add the butter, iodized salt, black pepper, garlic powder, and 1/2 cup of evaporated milk. Mash until smooth (there may be some lumps, and that's OK!). Add more evaporated milk until the potatoes reach the desired consistency—they should be soft but hold peaks (not too soft or squishy). Spoon onto each plate. Add chicken and some sauce. ■

I was just putting "stuff" in a slow cooker,
experimenting with what to make for dinner,
and ended up making this cacciatore,
which I didn't know it was called
until we had friends over for dinner one evening.
This recipe is so quick, easy, and tasty!
Grown-ups and children love it!
It's great for family meals as well as serving for company.
An alternate side dish: you can use
rice instead of mashed potatoes. —XE

Stephanie Thomson
Sugar Land, Texas

Asparagus & Onion
Chicken

Makes 4 servings

1 (1-pound) bag frozen carrots (either sliced or baby carrots)

4 to 6 boneless, skinless chicken breast halves

1 tablespoon Italian seasoning

1 (10-ounce) can condensed French onion soup

1 (10-ounce) can cream of asparagus or
cream of broccoli soup

1 teaspoon garlic powder

1/2 teaspoon black pepper

3/4 pound pasta of your choice, cooked

Place the carrots in the bottom of a 4-quart slow cooker. Add the chicken and Italian seasoning. Add the French onion soup, cover, and cook on low for 5 to 6 hours. Add the cream of asparagus soup, garlic powder, and pepper and cook for another 15 to 20 minutes, until the cream soup dissolves well and makes a nice, creamy gravy. It is sometimes easier to dissolve the cream soup by removing the chicken (keep warm) first. Serve over pasta. ■

poultry dishes

Rosemary Stone
Punta Gorda, Florida

Green Curry Chicken

Makes 4 servings

2 pounds chicken thighs

1/2 (4-ounce) can green curry paste (found at Thai/Asian
foods shops), or to taste—it's extremely spicy hot!

1 (14-ounce) can coconut milk (not cream)

1 red bell pepper, sliced

1 green bell pepper, sliced

1 large sweet onion, sliced

1 cup jasmine rice or long-grain white rice, cooked,
for serving

Fresh basil leaves, for garnish

Place the chicken in a 4-quart slow cooker. Mix the green curry paste with a small amount of coconut milk. Add this and the remaining coconut milk to the chicken. Cover and cook on low for 5 to 6 hours. Add the peppers and onion and cook on high for 1 hour. Put the cooked rice on a platter, spoon the chicken and vegetables over the rice, and add as much sauce as you like. Or put the sauce in a gravy boat to serve at the table. Garnish with fresh basil. ■

Sharyl Ingham
Oakland, California

Drumstick Surprise

Makes 4 to 6 servings

1 cup diced carrots

1 cup diced celery

1 cup diced onion

2 tablespoons olive oil

Salt and black pepper

Paprika

Cayenne

6 chicken drumsticks (about 2 pounds)

1 1/2 cups brown rice, uncooked (not quick-cook or instant)

1 1/2 cups chicken broth, more or less, as needed

Sauté the carrots, celery, and onion in the oil in a large skillet over medium heat until soft, 5 to 7 minutes. Transfer to a 6-quart slow cooker. Mix the salt, black pepper, paprika, and cayenne to taste to make a rub. Rub the mixture all over the drumsticks and brown them on all sides in the same pan, 3 minutes per side. Layer the rice on the vegetables in the slow cooker; then layer on the drumsticks and pour in enough chicken broth just to cover the mixture. Cover and cook on low for 6 to 7 hours. ∎

poultry dishes

Lisa Kettell
Hackettstown, New Jersey

Sassy
Chicken Balsamic

Makes 4 to 6 servings

6 skinless, boneless chicken breasts

1/4 cup extra virgin olive oil

5 cloves garlic, chopped

2 cups water

2 chicken bouillon cubes

1/3 cup white wine

1 large Vidalia or red onion, chopped

1 large red bell pepper, thinly sliced

1 small hot pepper, sliced (optional)

1/2 cup chopped mushrooms

1 tablespoon drained capers

1/2 cup Kalamata olives, pitted and chopped

1/2 teaspoon dried basil

1/2 teaspoon salt, plus more for seasoning

1 cup balsamic vinegar

Cooked pasta or rice, for serving

1/4 cup freshly grated Parmesan cheese

Black pepper

Cut the chicken into cubes and set aside. In a medium sauté pan, heat the olive oil over medium heat, add half of the garlic, and sauté for 1 minute. Add the chicken and sauté for 2 minutes on each side; remove from the heat. Put the water in a microwave-safe measuring cup, add the bouillon cubes, and heat in the microwave for 2 minutes, or until the bouillon cubes dissolve.

Add the sautéed chicken with the oil to a 5-quart slow cooker. In a separate medium bowl, combine the warmed broth and the wine, stir, and pour over the chicken. Cover and cook on high for 1 hour. Add the rest of the garlic, the onion, peppers, mushrooms, capers, olives, basil, salt, and vinegar and stir. Turn the heat down to low and cook for 4 to 5 hours, stirring occasionally.

Remove the chicken from the slow cooker. If a thicker sauce is desired, dissolve 1/3 cup all-purpose flour in 1/3 cup water. Stir into the slow cooker, cover, and cook on high for 30 minutes. Serve over pasta or rice, then sprinkle with the Parmesan and season with salt and pepper to taste.

{continued}

poultry dishes

Sassy
Chicken Balsamic
{continued}

If you don't have a slow cooker or would like to shorten the cooking time, replace the slow cooker with a 4- to 6-quart saucepan or Dutch oven and cook, covered, for 45 minutes over medium heat, stirring every 5 minutes. ∎

My grandfather's parents came here from Italy and exposed me to Italian cooking. My grandmothers went to the store only when they needed something and never wasted anything. They always made recipes from scratch, from tomato sauce with three meats to my grandmother's balsamic chicken. She'd throw every ingredient she had in a large pot and cook it all day. It was the most tender and delicious meal! I tried to perfect her recipe, and this is the result. —LK

Irene Pappas Edwards
St. Louis, Missouri

Turkey Tenderloin
with Butter Glaze

Makes 8 servings

2 large turkey tenderloins, about 2 pounds

1/2 pound (2 sticks) salted butter, cold

1 teaspoon salt

1 teaspoon rubbed sage

1 tablespoon raw sugar

Place the tenderloins in a 4-quart slow cooker. Cut up the butter and spread it evenly on the turkey. Season with salt, sage, and sugar. Cover and cook on low for 5 to 7 hours. Slice and top with the glaze before serving. Great with mashed potatoes and steamed broccoli or broccolini. ■

I just stumbled on this while experimenting with the slow cooker. The meat is very tender, and you can use the butter glaze for your sides—corn, potatoes, vegetables, pasta. It's always a favorite with the kids because this meat is succulent and flavorful. Besides, everything is better with butter! The leftovers make great sandwiches! —IPE

poultry dishes

Heidi Woodruff
Coos Bay, Oregon

Heidi's
Turkey Lasagna
& Easy Bread Sticks

Makes 4 to 6 servings

1 pound ground turkey

1 tablespoon olive oil, if needed

1 pound mozzarella cheese, shredded

3 cups ricotta cheese

1/2 cup freshly grated Parmesan cheese

2 eggs

2 tablespoons dried parsley flakes

1 teaspoon salt

1/2 teaspoon black pepper

1 (26-ounce) jar spaghetti sauce of your choice

1 (9-ounce) package no-boil flat lasagna noodles

Butter-flavored cooking spray

1 loaf frozen bread dough, thawed

Salt, black pepper, dried parsley, dried basil, and dried
        oregano for the bread sticks

Brown the ground turkey in the olive oil (if needed to prevent sticking) in a large skillet over medium heat, 8 to 10 minutes; drain and set aside. In a large bowl, mix together all but 1/2 cup of the mozzarella, the ricotta, Parmesan, eggs, 2 tablespoons dried parsley flakes, 1 teaspoon salt, and 1/2 teaspoon black pepper. Set aside.

Spray a 6-quart slow cooker with nonstick spray. In the bowl of a 6-quart slow cooker, spread about 1 cup of the spaghetti sauce, or enough to coat the bottom. Divide the noodles, cooked turkey, cheese mixture, and remaining spaghetti sauce into 3 portions. Layer each of them in that order in the slow cooker. Top with the reserved 1/2 cup of mozzarella. Cover and cook on low for 5 to 6 hours, or until the noodles are softened and the mixture is cooked through.

To make the bread sticks, preheat the oven to 375°F. Spray a baking sheet with the butter-flavored spray. Cut the thawed dough into 8 sections. Roll each piece between your hands until it's about 6 inches long. Place the sticks on the baking sheet and spray them liberally with the spray. Sprinkle the tops with the seasonings to taste and bake for 15 minutes, or until golden. ■

First we eat,
then we do everything else.

—M.F.K. Fisher

Pork
Dishes

Denise McCoy

West Harrison, Indiana

Simple Tangy, Sweet & Moist
Pork Roast

Makes 6 to 8 servings

1 (approximately 3-pound) boneless pork loin

1/4 cup spicy brown mustard

1 1/2 cups firmly packed light brown sugar,
  or more or less to taste

Rub the pork loin with the mustard until the roast is completely coated. Pack the brown sugar on the pork loin on top of the mustard until the roast is thoroughly coated with brown sugar. Don't rub it on; pack it on, so it stays on the roast. You will find you may want to use more or less of the mustard or brown sugar. This is a "to your taste" recipe, so there is no set amount or right or wrong. As long as the pork loin is coated with the mustard and brown sugar, it will cook perfectly. Place the pork in a 5-quart slow cooker. Cover and cook on low for 6 to 8 hours or on high for 3 to 4 hours. Even though no liquid was added, the roast will be tender and moist and have a wonderful tangy/sweet flavor. The meat and brown sugar and mustard create their own juice as the meat cooks. Take the meat out and let rest before slicing. Slice as thick as you like. Return the meat to its juice in the slow cooker set on warm until ready to serve. ■

Dawn Anderson
Colorado Springs, Colorado

Green Chile
Pork Roast

Makes 6 to 8 servings

1 (3-pound) pork (or beef) roast

2 (4-ounce) cans diced green chiles

2 tablespoons minced garlic

1 medium onion, chopped

Place the roast in a 5-quart slow cooker. Add the chiles, garlic, and onion. Cover and cook on low for 6 to 8 hours or overnight. Remove the meat, shred it with two forks, and return it to the cooker. Let cook for 1 hour without the lid to cook off some liquid; drain a little of the excess off. ■

With seven kids and some new in-laws, this makes an easy and delicious Sunday dinner. We serve the meat with tortillas, cheese, tomatoes, lettuce, and all the other fixings for a Mexican meal. It's so easy even my kids can make it. —DA

pork dishes

Cheryl Goode-MacKinnon
Dearborn, Michigan

Autumn
Pork Roast

Makes 6 to 8 servings

1 (3-pound) pork loin or about 6 pork chops,
      preferably thick

2 tablespoons oil (optional)

1 (24-ounce) jar applesauce

2 to 3 cups apple juice

1/4 to 1/3 cup soy sauce

1 to 2 tablespoons brown sugar

1 tablespoon butter

For best full flavor, brown the pork in the oil in a skillet over medium-high heat. If you don't have time, you can skip this step. Put the pork in a 5-quart slow cooker. Mix the applesauce, apple juice, and soy sauce to taste in a bowl. Pour over the meat, cover, and cook on low for 6 to 8 hours. About three-quarters of the way through the cooking, add the brown sugar to taste and butter on top of the meat. Serve with rice and veggies. This is even better the following day. ■

My daughter put this recipe together originally with just the pork, applesauce, and soy sauce, but I was making it one day and did not have enough applesauce, so I substituted the juice. Voilà—it was fantastic. —CG-M

Barbara Bulmer
Barrie, Ontario, Canada

English Pork Roast

Makes 6 to 8 servings

1 (3- to 5-pound) boneless pork roast
    (a cheap cut is OK if you trim the fat)
1 (1-ounce) envelope dry onion soup mix
2 or 3 cloves garlic, minced, to taste
1 1/2 cups apple juice or 1 (12-ounce) bottle imported
    English cider (if available at the liquor store)
Freshly ground black pepper

Place all the ingredients in a 6-quart slow cooker in the order listed. Cover and cook on low for 7 to 9 hours or on high for 3 to 5 hours. The meat will be so tender that it just falls apart. You may wish to skim off any fat and use the juices to dribble over each serving. Serve with mashed potatoes, steamed carrots, and crusty bread. Great for a fall Sunday dinner. ■

This recipe was given to me by a neighbor's mother who lived in England. I had to adapt it to our measurements and enhance it to our taste and flavor likes. She had other ingredients that we didn't care for (bay leaves, thyme, and rosemary). I feel it's now my own. Leftovers make great sandwiches. —BB

pork dishes

119

Nansi N. Vos
Avon, Minnesota

Nana Nansi's
Pork in a Pot

Makes 4 to 6 servings

1 1/2 cups carrots in 1-inch pieces

2 medium onions, cut into eighths

1 1/2 cups celery in 3/4-inch pieces

1/2 pound green beans, cut into 2-inch pieces

2 pounds boneless pork shoulder, cut into 1 1/2-inch pieces

3 tablespoons all-purpose flour

2 teaspoons salt

1/4 teaspoon ground ginger

1/8 teaspoon hot red pepper flakes

1/2 cup ketchup

Place the carrots in the bottom of a 5-quart slow cooker. Layer on the onions and then the celery, green beans, and pork. Combine the flour, salt, ginger, and red pepper flakes in a small bowl. Add the ketchup and mix well. Spoon the mixture over the meat, making a seal around the edges. Cover the slow cooker and cook on high for 3 to 4 hours or on low for 7 to 10 hours, or until the meat and vegetables are tender. ■

Suzanne Veazey
Weddington, North Carolina

BBQ Pork

Makes 6 servings

1 (14-ounce) bottle ketchup

1 1/4 cups water

1/4 cup vinegar

3 tablespoons brown sugar

1 tablespoon dry mustard

3 tablespoons Worcestershire sauce

2 teaspoons chili powder

Pinch of ground cloves

Pinch of garlic powder

1 (3- to 4-pound) Boston butt pork roast

Combine all the ingredients except the pork; mix well. Place the pork in a 5-quart slow cooker. Pour 2 cups of the sauce over the pork and turn the meat to coat it all over. Cover and cook on low for 7 to 8 hours or high for 4 to 5 hours or until the meat pulls easily from the bone. Use a fork to shred the cooled pork and serve with the remaining sauce. ■

pork dishes

Debbie Wadley
Pleasant Grove, Utah

Sweet Pork

Makes 10 to 12 servings

Vegetable oil cooking spray

4 pounds boneless pork roast

2 (8-ounce) cans tomato sauce

1 teaspoon pressed garlic

1 1/2 cups firmly packed brown sugar

2 teaspoons ground cumin

2 cups Dr. Pepper

2 tablespoons molasses

1/2 teaspoon salt

Black pepper

Spray a 6-quart slow cooker with nonstick spray. Place the roast in the slow cooker set on low. Mix the remaining ingredients and stir until the sugar dissolves. Pour over the meat, cover, and cook on low until the meat is tender and pulls away with a fork, 6 to 8 hours or overnight. When ready to serve, remove the liquid, shred the pork with a fork, and then add about 2 cups of the liquid back. Great for taco salad, burritos, or on a bun. ■

Susan Ego
Corte Madera, California

Mexi-Pork

Makes 8 to 10 servings

1 (3 1/2-pound) pork shoulder, excess fat trimmed

1 (10-ounce) can mild green enchilada sauce

1 (4-ounce) can diced green chiles

1 clove garlic, minced

1 medium red onion, sliced

1/3 cup fresh lime juice

1/2 cup chopped fresh cilantro

Dash of salt

Dash of black pepper

Tortillas, warmed, for serving

Place the pork in a 4-quart slow cooker. Combine the enchilada sauce, chiles, garlic, and onion; spoon the sauce over the pork. Cover and cook on low for 7 to 9 hours, until the pork is very tender. Transfer the pork to a cutting board. Break the pork into bite-sized pieces with a spoon and return them to the slow cooker. Mix in the lime juice, cilantro, and salt and pepper to taste; stir to combine. To serve, spoon the pork mixture onto warmed tortillas, fold, and eat. ■

pork dishes

Tammy Gilley
Sherwood, Oregon

Very Verde Carnitas

Makes 8 servings

1 tablespoon olive oil

1 medium yellow onion, diced

2 cloves garlic, minced

1 teaspoon dried oregano

1/2 teaspoon ground cumin

1/2 teaspoon ground coriander

1/2 teaspoon salt

1/4 teaspoon freshly ground black pepper

1 (4 1/2-pound) boneless pork roast

1 (16-ounce) jar green chile salsa

8 burrito-size flour tortillas

2 (15-ounce) cans black beans, drained and rinsed

1 cup grated cheddar cheese

Sour cream and chopped fresh cilantro, for garnish

In a large skillet, heat the olive oil over medium heat. Add the onion and garlic and cook, stirring often, until transparent, 4 to 5 minutes. Place the cooked onion in a 5-quart slow cooker. In a small bowl, combine the oregano, cumin, coriander, salt, and pepper. Rub the seasonings into the pork roast. Place the pork roast into the skillet and sear on all sides to seal in the juices, 12 to 15 minutes. Place the roast on top of the onions in the slow cooker. Pour in the salsa. Cover and cook on low for 6 to 8 hours, until the pork is very tender.

Warm the tortillas. Heat the black beans in a saucepan on the stove. Using two forks, shred the pork roast, then mix the meat with the cooked onion and salsa. For each burrito, spread a tortilla with about 1/2 cup of the warmed beans. Top with 1 cup of the shredded pork and onions. Roll the burrito and garnish with cheddar cheese, sour cream, and cilantro. Repeat with the remaining tortillas. Enjoy! ■

This is a lip-smackin', easy-to-prepare meal! I love to throw the ingredients into my slow cooker in the morning, and by the time I get home from work, it smells like my mom's been cooking in my kitchen all day. Talk about comfort food! —JG

pork dishes

Nan Slaughter
Sammamish, Washington

Cuban
Pork Sandwiches
with Cilantro Aïoli

Makes 8 to 10 servings

2 large yellow onions, thinly sliced

1 (4- to 5-pound) Boston butt pork roast, fat left on

2 tablespoons vegetable oil

1 teaspoon ground cumin

1 teaspoon salt

1 teaspoon freshly ground black pepper

3 cloves garlic, minced

1 teaspoon dried oregano

1 cup orange juice

Juice of 1 lime

2 tablespoons chopped fresh cilantro

1 tablespoon brown sugar

Cilantro Aïoli

1 cup mayonnaise

1 cup plain yogurt

2 tablespoons fresh lemon juice

3 tablespoons chopped fresh cilantro

1 teaspoon minced garlic

2 French baguettes, halved lengthwise

Romaine lettuce for topping

Place half of the onions in the bottom of a 6-quart slow cooker and turn the setting to high. Brown the roast on all sides in the oil in a skillet over medium-high heat, 12 to 15 minutes. Transfer to the slow cooker. Add the remaining onions on top of the pork roast. In a bowl, combine the cumin, salt, pepper, garlic, oregano, orange juice, lime juice, cilantro, and brown sugar. Mix well and then pour over the pork. Put the lid on and cook on low for 6 to 8 hours. When the pork is done, it will be practically falling apart. Drain the liquid and shred the pork with a fork.

Combine all the ingredients for the cilantro aïoli in a small bowl and mix well. To assemble the sandwiches, generously coat both sides of the sliced baguettes with the cilantro aïoli. Place the shredded pork on the baguettes and top with romaine. Slice the baguettes into sandwich-size servings. ■

This is a family favorite. We always have it on Halloween, right before trick-or-treating, and everyone always asks for this recipe! —NS

Patricia Caccia
St. Petersburg, Florida

Apple-Picking-Time
Pork Chops

Makes 4 to 6 servings

6 to 8 boneless pork chops, about 1 inch thick

1/2 teaspoon kosher salt

1/2 teaspoon black pepper

3 tablespoons brown sugar

1 1/2 teaspoons ground cinnamon

6 medium Granny Smith apples, peeled, cored,
and quartered

Sprinkle the pork chops with salt and pepper and place in a 4-quart slow cooker. Combine the brown sugar and cinnamon and sprinkle evenly over the chops. Place the apples on top of the chops. Cover and cook on low for 5 to 7 hours. ■

My aunt Maryann was from Lancaster, Pennsylvania, and cooked many Amish-inspired dishes. She used applesauce after browning the chops in a skillet. I adapted this recipe for the slow cooker by using whole apples. This is one of my family's favorite dinners. I serve them with baked sweet potato fries and a salad. —PC

Patricia Cook

Duncanville, Texas

Reuben Pork Chops

Makes 4 servings

4 (1-inch-thick) butterflied pork chops (about 1 1/2
  pounds)

2 tablespoons oil

1 (32-ounce) jar sauerkraut

1 (8-ounce) bottle Thousand Island dressing

2 cups shredded Swiss cheese

Brown the pork chops on both sides in the oil in a skillet over medium-high heat, 8 to 10 minutes. Transfer the pork chops to a 4-quart slow cooker. Layer the sauerkraut (drain off some of the liquid, but not all) over the pork chops. Cover with the entire bottle of salad dressing. Cover and cook on low for 5 to 7 hours. Sprinkle the top with cheese during the last hour of cooking. ∎

The browning of the pork chops before placing them in the slow cooker is important—it adds to the flavor and appearance of the meal! —PC

pork dishes

Doe West
Webster, Massachusetts

Autumn Harvest
Sampler

Makes 2 to 4 servings

6 medium carrots, cut in half

12 Yukon Gold potatoes, peeled and halved (about 2 1/2
pounds)

2 sweet onions, quartered

4 (1-inch-thick) pork chops

2 Granny Smith apples, peeled, cored, and quartered

1 (10-ounce) can condensed cream of celery soup

1 can water

Salt and black pepper

Just a kiss of ground cinnamon

Layer the carrots in the bottom of a 6-quart slow cooker. Top with the potatoes and onions. Lay the pork chops on top of the veggies. Now layer on the apples. Pour the can of cream of celery soup over it all and then a can of water swirled in the can first to get any last bit of the soup. Season with salt, pepper, and cinnamon to taste. Set on low, cover, and cook for 6 to 8 hours while you have a wonderful day! Come home hungry and serve up a simple, delicious meal with hot apple cider stirred with a cinnamon stick to celebrate the harvest. ■

I am known for walking into the kitchen and simply opening cabinets and creating a meal from what is at hand. My favorite season is autumn, and one morning I came out to the scent of newly picked apples, the sun shining on some Yukon Gold potatoes, and the memory of plump pork chops from the butcher shop sitting in paper in the refrigerator. They merged in my mind, and I could "taste" the harvest bounty. —DW

pork dishes

Claudia Vergamini
Council Bluffs, Iowa

Ham & Potatoes

Makes 6 to 8 servings

About 1 pound ham (such as leftover spiral cut,

      turkey ham, boneless ham), cut into about 8 slices

8 medium potatoes, peeled and sliced

1/4 cup chopped onion

1 cup shredded sharp cheddar cheese

1 (10-ounce) can condensed cream of mushroom soup

Paprika, for sprinkling (optional)

Spray a 5-quart slow cooker with nonstick spray. Put a layer of ham, potatoes, onion, and cheese in the bottom. Repeat the layers. Spoon the soup over the top. Sprinkle with paprika if you like it. Cover and cook on low for 5 to 7 hours. ■

*This is a very easy winter meal,
and it's so different from
your typical ham and potatoes casserole!* —CV

Geralyn Powers
Lyman, Wyoming

Pork & White Beans

Makes 8 servings

2 pounds boneless pork roast

2 (15-ounce) cans white beans, such as cannelini or navy,
    with liquid

1 (10-ounce) can diced tomatoes with green chiles

1/2 cup chopped onion

1 tablespoon chicken soup base (not bouillon)

1/2 cup sour cream

1/2 cup grated cheese

Combine the pork, beans, tomatoes, onion, and chicken soup base in a 5-quart slow cooker, cover, and cook on high for 3 to 4 hours or low for 7 to 8 hours. Shred the pork before serving, which should be easy as it falls apart at this point. Serve with a dollop of sour cream and grated cheese. ■

Our family loves this delicious, hearty stew.
It is quick and simple to prepare and is high in protein
for those watching calories. The tomatoes and green chile
peppers give it a little zesty zing! —GP

pork dishes

Nancy Foster
Arnold, Missouri

Boilermaker Wurst

Makes 6 servings

2 medium yellow onions, halved and thickly sliced

6 links fresh bratwurst or knockwurst

12 new small yellow or red potatoes

1 (12-ounce) bottle beer

1/3 cup whiskey or bourbon

2 to 4 cups water

Cracked black pepper and kosher salt

6 cups fresh spinach (optional)

Separate the slices of onion and cover the bottom of a 5-quart slow cooker with them. Add the wurst on top, then the potatoes. Pour in the beer, whiskey, and enough water to just cover the potatoes. Set the slow cooker on low, cover, and cook for 6 to 8 hours.

Just before serving, transfer the sausages and potatoes to serving dishes. Season the potatoes with pepper and salt to taste. Strain out the onions with a slotted spoon and put in a serving dish. Heat a large skillet over high heat. Add 1/4 cup of the liquid from the slow cooker. Toss in the spinach leaves, and cook for 4 minutes or until they just begin to wilt. Sprinkle to taste with pepper and salt. Transfer to a bowl and serve immediately. Best accompanied by horseradish, spicy mustard, and crusty rye bread. ∎

Our family had a dear friend who was a boilermaker. He always had beer in hand and one in his pocket to share, and he still had enough to add to every meal, whether barbecue, soup, or pork chops.

This dish is a special treat for supper.

The smell fills the house and our hearts with warm memories. Our boilermaker friend was allergic to wheat, so he would substitute a big pile of butter beans for the bread. They make this meal especially satisfying. —NF

pork dishes

Theresa Norsky
Cohocton, New York

Opa's
Sauerkraut & Wurst

Makes 6 to 8 servings

1 medium onion, cut into thin half rings

8 tablespoons (1 stick) butter or margarine

1 tablespoon caraway seeds

6 to 10 juniper berries, to taste

1 (28- to 32-ounce) can or bag sauerkraut, drained

1 cup applesauce (homemade is best)

1 (12-ounce) bottle beer

6 to 12 hot dogs, or smoked brats, or sausages, depending
on your preferences

Kummelweck rolls or thick pretzels, for serving

Sauté the onion in the butter in a large skillet over medium heat until caramelized and soft, about 15 minutes. Then add the caraway seeds, juniper berries, and sauerkraut. Once everything is bubbling hot, stir in the applesauce and beer. Then arrange in a 5-quart slow cooker a layer of sauerkraut, followed by a layer of wursts, then kraut, then wurst. Cover and cook for 4 to 6 hours. Serve with kummelweck rolls or hot thick pretzels and, of course, beer. *Prosit!* ■

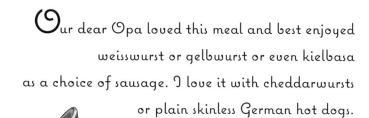

Our dear Opa loved this meal and best enjoyed weisswurst or gelbwurst or even kielbasa as a choice of sausage. I love it with cheddarwursts or plain skinless German hot dogs. And of course you have to wash it down with a radlermass (German beer with lemon-lime soda). —TN

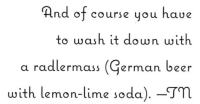

pork dishes

Joyce Ingalls

North Hollywood, California

Veggies & Dogs
the Kids Will Love

Makes 4 to 6 servings

1 tablespoon minced garlic (3 cloves)

2 tablespoons ketchup

2 cups chicken broth, canned or homemade

2 tablespoons orange marmalade

1 tablespoon mild curry powder

2 tablespoons dried parsley flakes

1/2 teaspoon kosher salt, or to taste

4 cups cauliflower in bite-sized pieces (1 small head)

2 cups peeled potatoes in 1/2-inch dice

1 cup green bell pepper in 1/2-inch dice (1 medium)

2 cups carrots in 1/2-inch dice

1/2 cup onion in 1/2-inch dice (1 small)

1 cup frozen cut green beans, rinsed to thaw

1 (15-ounce) can garbanzo beans (chickpeas),
        drained and rinsed

1 (15-ounce) can whole kernel corn, drained and rinsed

1 cup frozen peas, thawed

6 hot dogs, cut into 1/4-inch coins

Steamed rice or egg noodles, for serving

Place the garlic, ketchup, chicken broth, marmalade, curry powder, dried parsley, and salt in a 6-quart slow cooker. Stir to blend. Add the cauliflower, potatoes, green pepper, carrots, onion, green beans, garbanzos, and corn. Cover and cook on low for 6 to 7 hours, or until the potatoes and carrots are tender. Hint: Do not open the lid while dinner is cooking. Every time you open the lid it takes the slow cooker 20 minutes to recover its cooking temperature. When the vegetables are done, turn off the cooker and add the thawed peas and hot dog rounds. Gently stir everything together. Replace the lid and let sit for 15 minutes. Serve with steamed rice or egg noodles. ∎

Like many children, my two boys needed encouragement to try new vegetables. I started making this vegetable/hot dog stew with just potatoes, carrots, peas, and corn— the surefire winners with kids. Over time I added a new vegetable, then another and another. It must have worked, because both boys grew up thinking veggies are a winner. —JJ

pork dishes

Allison Kanagy
Arlington, Texas

Spicy
Black-Eyed Peas
with Sausage & Ham

Makes 6 to 8 servings

2 slices thick-cut bacon, sliced into 3/4-inch pieces

5 cloves garlic, pressed

1 large onion, chopped

1/4 cup finely diced bell pepper

1 fresh jalapeño pepper, seeded and finely chopped

1 fresh poblano pepper, seeded and finely chopped

2 tablespoons Cajun roux (jarred or homemade)

2 cups water

1/4 cup chicken soup base

1 quart chicken stock

1 to 2 pounds ham and/or sausage chunks

1 teaspoon cayenne

1/4 bunch fresh thyme leaves

2 teaspoons kosher salt

2 teaspoons freshly ground black pepper

Juice of 1 lemon

2 tablespoons tomato paste

2 bay leaves

1 pound dried black-eyed peas

4 green onions, chopped

1/4 cup finely chopped fresh parsley

Cook the bacon in a skillet over medium-low heat. Transfer the bacon to a paper towel-lined plate, leaving the rendered fat in the skillet. Add the garlic, onion, bell pepper, jalapeño pepper, and poblano pepper to the fat in the skillet and sauté on medium-high heat for about 5 minutes. Stir in the roux, then the water, chicken base, and chicken stock. Bring to a simmer, stirring constantly. Transfer to a 6-quart slow cooker. Add the ham, cayenne, thyme, salt, black pepper, and lemon juice and mix well. Stir in the tomato paste, bay leaves, and dried black-eyed peas. Cover and simmer on high for 6 hours. You can add the bacon to the slow cooker an hour before serving or when you serve it. Cooking the bacon with the peas will add a little extra flavor, but adding it at the end maintains its texture. About 20 minutes before serving, stir in the green onions and parsley. ■

This is a nice variation on red beans and rice. Black-eyed peas are tasty and nutritious, and these spicy peas are great with corn bread. —AX

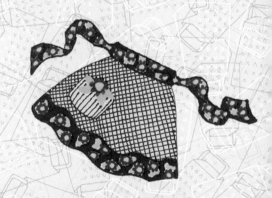

A cook is creative,
marrying ingredients
in the way a poet
marries words.

—Roger Verge

Side
Dishes

Sharman Pittman
Asheville, North Carolina

Bean Pot

Makes 4 to 6 servings

1 (15-ounce) can butter beans, drained

1 (15-ounce) can kidney beans, drained

1 (15-ounce) can baked beans, with liquid

1/2 cup ketchup

1/2 cup finely chopped onion

1/2 cup firmly packed brown sugar

1/3 cup finely chopped green bell pepper

1 1/2 pounds ham, diced

2 cups shredded cheddar cheese

Combine all the ingredients except the cheese in a 5-quart slow cooker. Cover and cook on low for 3 to 4 hours. Serve in bowls topped with shredded cheddar cheese. The recipe is easily doubled for a larger crowd. ■

This comfort food is a great dish during the cold winter. The smell created while cooking is heavenly throughout the house. Bean Pot can be served with a salad and warm cheese bread or corn bread for a complete meal. —SP

Maureen Kersten
Gillett, Wisconsin

Grandpa's
Calico Beans

Makes 6 servings

1 pound ground beef

Salt, black pepper, and a dash of celery salt for seasoning

1 pound bacon

1 cup chopped onion

1/2 cup ketchup

3/4 cup firmly packed brown sugar

1/4 cup granulated sugar

1 tablespoon salt

1 tablespoon prepared mustard

3 tablespoons white vinegar

2 (15-ounce) cans pork and beans

1 (15-ounce) can lima beans, drained

1 (15-ounce) can butter beans, drained

1 (15-ounce) can dark red kidney beans, drained

Brown the ground beef, seasoned with salt, pepper, and celery salt, in a skillet over medium-high heat; drain. Wipe out the skillet and fry the bacon on medium-low until crisp; drain and crumble. Put all the ingredients in a 6-quart slow cooker and mix gently. Cover and cook on low for 2 to 4 hours. To fill up the slow cooker for gatherings, use 2 cans each of the lima, butter, and kidney beans. ■

side dishes

Glenda Jacobs
Norwalk, California

Good Ole Fashun
Pinto Beans

Makes 4 servings (about 8 cups)

1 (16-ounce) package dried pinto beans, sorted and rinsed

4 to 6 slices bacon, cut in half

1 medium onion, peeled

1 tablespoon salt or Mrs. Dash seasoning, or to taste

Put the beans in a 5-quart slow cooker and add cool water to cover. Add the bacon pieces and the onion. Cover and cook on low for 6 hours. The beans will turn a delightful shade of red when done and will be soft enough to mash if desired. Add salt to taste only after the beans are cooked through. ■

I am Native American and grew up on a large pot of beans slowly cooking on the stove all day. When I got married and began my own family, I did not have time to babysit the pot of beans like my mother did, so one day I set up my slow cooker. These are a great starter for any meal, such as a traditional American Indian meal of "fry bread," rice, beans with seasoned (cooked) ground beef sprinkled on top, and a slice of juicy watermelon. —GJ

Mindy LittleCook
Ponca City, Oklahoma

Three-Bean Hot Dish

Makes 6 to 8 servings

1 pound bacon

1 pound ground beef

1 (15-ounce) can lima beans, with liquid

2 (15-ounce) cans kidney beans, with liquid

1 (15-ounce) can black-eyed peas, with liquid

1 tablespoon white vinegar

1/2 cup ketchup

1/2 cup firmly packed brown sugar

1 cup chopped yellow onion

Fry the bacon in a medium skillet until slightly crisp; set aside to cool on a paper towel. Wipe out the skillet and brown the ground beef over medium-high heat; drain and set aside. Pour the cans of beans into a 6-quart slow cooker. Add the vinegar, ketchup, and brown sugar. Crumble the bacon and add. Then add the beef and chopped onion. Stir, cover, and cook on low for 5 to 7 hours or on high for 2 hours. ∎

I got this recipe years ago from my Swedish family in Wisconsin. It's not a traditional Swedish dish, but it is a family favorite. We enjoy it with homemade bread, soda crackers, and even fry bread or white rice. —MLC

side dishes

Jill Rosell
Springfield, Missouri

Old Settlers Beans

Makes 6 to 8 servings

1 pound ground beef

1/2 pound bacon, chopped

1 onion, chopped

1/4 cup firmly packed brown sugar

1/4 cup granulated sugar

1/4 cup ketchup

1/4 cup barbecue sauce

1 tablespoon prepared mustard

2 tablespoons molasses

1/2 to 1 teaspoon chili powder

1 teaspoon salt

1/2 teaspoon black pepper

1/4 teaspoon garlic powder

1 (16-ounce) can dark red kidney beans, drained

1 (15-ounce) can large butter beans, drained

1 (15-ounce) can pork and beans

Brown the ground beef in a skillet over medium-high heat, 8 to 10 minutes, and drain. Wipe out the skillet and cook the bacon over medium-low heat until crisp. Transfer to paper towels to drain, leaving the drippings in the skillet. Cook the onion in the bacon drippings

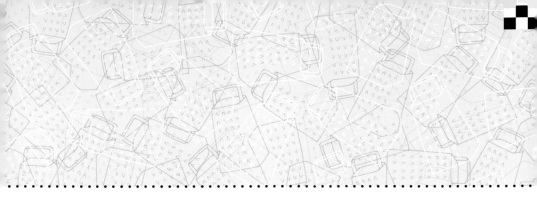

until tender, 4 to 5 minutes. Put the beef, bacon, and onions in a 6-quart slow cooker and add the sugars, ketchup, barbecue sauce, mustard, molasses, chili powder, salt, pepper, garlic powder, and beans. Cover and cook on low for 6 to 8 hours or on high for 3 to 4 hours. ■

This is a very easy and tasty dish. It is great for picnics, potlucks, and winter evenings. It is tasty served warm or cold. It can be simmered on the stovetop, baked in the oven, or cooked in the slow cooker. It is also wonderful to fix while out camping. —JR

side dishes

Jerri Garofalo
Midlothian, Virginia

GiGi's Creamy
Zucchini Dish

Makes 4 to 6 servings

4 medium zucchini, sliced into 1/2-inch-thick rounds

3 cups water

1/4 cup (2-ounces) cream cheese, cubed

1 cup lightly crushed round buttery crackers

1/4 teaspoon salt

A few dashes of onion or garlic powder (optional)

Put the zucchini and water in a 5-quart slow cooker, cover, and cook on high for 1 to 2 hours, or until tender. Transfer the zucchini from the slow cooker to a colander and leave it there for 1 minute to drain well. Return the zucchini to the slow cooker and, using a potato masher, gently begin to mash the cooked zucchini. You will notice that it will release a lot of water or juice, but do not drain this off again. Add the cream cheese to the slow cooker and continue mashing and stirring to combine the ingredients. As soon as the mixture begins to turn creamy, add the crackers and blend and fluff just until combined. The crackers should soak up the moisture and be blended in, but don't overmix. Season to taste with salt and onion or garlic powder.

Once the dish is complete, turn the slow cooker to low for 1 to 2 hours. The slow cooker will keep the dish hot during serving on a cookout table, at a potluck, or at another party. This recipe is easy to double or to make in larger portions, and you can cook it on top of the stove too. ■

I created this recipe during a very abundant zucchini summer. It was an instant hit and has been a family favorite ever since. It is one vegetable dish I know that everyone will eat and ask for more. Yes, even the little ones. I always make sure I double or triple my recipe to accommodate second helpings and to have leftovers. Even my husband asks if we have leftovers of it. This goes great with grilled or roasted meats. And it's also a wonderful dish for vegetarians. I have replaced the cream cheese with a vegan cream cheese substitute, and no one knew the difference. Many years later it is still asked for at family dinners. The only difference is that now my grandchildren are asking for GiGi's Zucchini Dish too. —JG

Allison Kanagy
Arlington, Texas

Cabbage Rolls

Makes 6 to 8 servings

Sauce

1 teaspoon butter

1/2 cup chopped yellow onion

1/2 teaspoon minced garlic

1 (15-ounce) can diced tomatoes, with liquid

2 tablespoons tomato paste

1/2 teaspoon sugar

1/4 cup cream

3/4 cup chicken stock

1 tablespoon apple cider vinegar

1/4 teaspoon cayenne, Cajun, or Creole seasoning (optional)

Rolls

1 small head of cabbage, cored and scalded in boiling
       water until soft and easy to separate

1 teaspoon butter

1/2 cup chopped yellow onion

1 teaspoon chopped garlic

3/4 pound ground sirloin

1/2 pound ground pork

1/4 cup cream

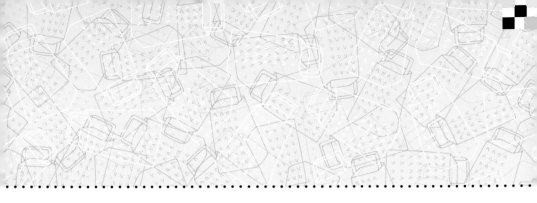

1/4 cup tomato paste

3 tablespoons freshly grated Parmesan cheese

2 tablespoons finely chopped fresh Italian (flat-leaf) parsley

3/4 cup cooked long-grain white rice

1 egg, slightly beaten

1 teaspoon Cajun/Creole seasoning

1/2 teaspoon salt

1 teaspoon black pepper

To make the sauce, melt the butter in a large skillet over medium heat. Add the onion and garlic and cook until soft, 5 to 7 minutes. Add the tomatoes with juice, tomato paste, and sugar and heat to a simmer. Add the cream, chicken stock, and vinegar. Taste here and, if you'd like, add 1/2 teaspoon of cayenne pepper or Cajun/Creole seasoning. You do not want to overwhelm with seasoning, but we do like it to be flavorful in both the sauce and the meat mixture. Remove the sauce from the heat and set it aside for now.

side dishes

{continued}

Cabbage Rolls

Separate the cabbage leaves and remove the hard spine from each leaf or shave it down to make the leaves easier to roll. Spread on paper towels and pat dry. Set aside, spine side down, on a work surface.

To make the stuffing, in a medium skillet melt the butter over medium-high heat. Add the onion and cook, stirring, until very wilted and starting to caramelize, about 5 minutes. Add the garlic and cook, stirring, for 1 minute. Remove from the heat and let cool slightly.

In a large bowl, combine the beef, pork, cream, tomato paste, Parmesan, parsley, rice, eggs, Cajun/Creole seasoning, salt, black pepper, and cooked onion and garlic. Mix well with a heavy wooden spoon or your hands. One at a time, spoon about 1/4 cup filling into the center of each cabbage leaf, depending on the size of the leaves. Roll each into a neat cylinder, folding the ends like an egg roll so that the stuffing is contained in the roll. Sometimes the shape of the cabbage leaf requires a lot of tucking to keep it closed. Once the rolls are placed in the cooker, they will be fine even if there is not a complete closure. I have a friend who instead

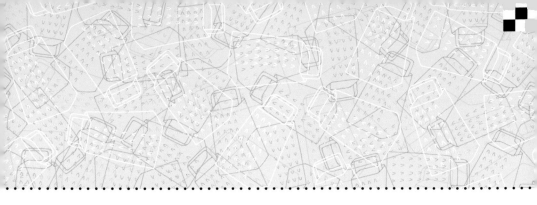

layers the meat, cabbage, and sauce like a lasagna, and it is perfectly delicious, too.

Line the bottom of a 6- or 7-quart slow cooker with the extra cabbage leaves; then place a layer of cabbage rolls in the slow cooker and cover with sauce. Repeat with the remaining ingredients, stacking the cabbage rolls as necessary. Pour more sauce over the rolls, put the lid on, and cook on high until the meat is cooked through and the rolls are tender, 6 to 8 hours. Turn to low to keep warm and serve the rolls with any remaining sauce spooned over the top if desired. ■

Cabbage rolls are very satisfying and worth the effort it takes to roll them up. The slow cooker makes cooking the rolls so easy. You can make enough for two dinners with this recipe. Always a winner! —AK

side dishes

Patricia Williams
Lake City, Florida

Unstuffed Cabbage

Makes 6 to 8 servings

1 pound ground turkey

1/2 cup dehydrated minced onion

2 cups quick-cooking white rice, uncooked

1 (28-ounce) can diced tomatoes, with liquid

1 small head of green cabbage

1 (64-ounce) bottle vegetable juice

Brown the ground turkey with the dried onion in a large skillet over medium heat, stirring and chopping with a spoon until cooked through and fine textured, 10 minutes. Transfer to a 6-quart slow cooker. Add the rice. Pour the tomatoes into a food processor and process just until mushy. Add to the cooker. Cut the head of cabbage into wedges, discarding the core. Slice the wedges into narrow strips and add to the cooker. Pour in the vegetable juice and stir. Cover and cook on high for about 4 hours, until the cabbage is tender. Serve in bowls. ■

I have always loved stuffed cabbage rolls, but they require a lot of work. One day I decided to try an easier way with my slow cooker and it turned out great. —PW

Lori Schankerman
Indianapolis, Indiana

Mediterranean
Stuffed Peppers

Makes 4 servings

4 large red or yellow bell peppers

1 (15-ounce) can cannellini beans, drained and rinsed

1/2 cup crumbled feta cheese

1/2 cup crumbled goat cheese

1/2 cup uncooked couscous

4 green onions, thinly sliced

1 garlic clove, minced

2 teaspoons dried oregano leaves

Salt and black pepper

1 tablespoon olive oil

Slice a thin layer from the base of each pepper so it sits flat. Slice off the top and discard the stem. Chop the tops and put them in a bowl. Remove the ribs and seeds from the peppers. Add the beans, feta, goat cheese, couscous, green onions, garlic, and oregano to the bowl. Season with salt and pepper and toss. Stuff the peppers with the bean mixture; place upright in a 5-quart slow cooker. Drizzle with olive oil, cover, and cook on high for 4 hours. ■

side dishes

I made this recipe for my daughter, who is a vegetarian and loves Mediterranean food. —LS

157

Silvina Pedemonte
Doral, Florida

Ratatouille

Makes 6 to 8 servings

1 medium eggplant

1/4 cup olive oil

1 medium onion, sliced

2 cloves garlic, minced

2 medium zucchini, sliced 1/2 inch thick

1 medium green bell pepper, thinly sliced

1 medium red bell pepper, thinly sliced

5 medium tomatoes, peeled and quartered,
     or 1 (28-ounce) can crushed tomatoes, drained

1/4 cup chopped fresh Italian (flat-leaf) parsley

1/2 teaspoon dried thyme leaves

2 teaspoons salt

1 teaspoon dried basil leaves

1/2 teaspoon black pepper

Peel the eggplant and cut into 1-inch cubes. Heat the oil in a large saucepan. Add the onion and garlic and cook over medium heat until almost tender, about 5 minutes. Add the eggplant, zucchini, and bell peppers. Cook and stir for 2 to 3 minutes. Transfer to a 6-quart slow cooker. Add the tomatoes, parsley, and dry seasonings. Stir. Cover and cook on low 6 to 8 hours. Serve as a vegetable or a sauce for spaghetti. ■

Linda Cummings
Murfreesboro, Tennessee

Easy & Delicious
Creamed Corn

Makes 6 to 8 servings

1 (16-ounce) bag frozen corn (whole niblets)

1 (8-ounce) package cream cheese, cubed

8 tablespoons (1 stick) butter or margarine

Salt and black pepper (optional)

Combine the corn, cream cheese, and butter in a 3- to 5-quart slow cooker. Cover and cook on high for 30 minutes, or until the cream cheese and butter are melted, stirring well. Reduce the heat to low and cook for 1 to 3 hours. ■

This is a family favorite. It can easily be halved or doubled, depending on the number of people to be served. It can be cooked in the slow cooker, on the stove, or in the microwave. —LC

side dishes

159

Janelle Schaeffer
Surprise, Arizona

Corn Puddin'

Makes 6 servings

8 tablespoons (1 stick) butter, melted

1 (15-ounce) can creamed corn

1 (15-ounce) can whole kernel corn, drained

1 cup sour cream

1 egg, slightly beaten

1 cup shredded cheese (whatever kind you love!)

1 (7-ounce) box corn bread mix

Pinch of salt

Dash of black pepper

Fire up a 5-quart slow cooker, set on low, and melt the butter (because all really great recipes start with butter, right?), about 30 minutes. Add the cans of corn and the sour cream, which will cool the mixture down enough to add the egg, cheese, and corn bread mix. Season with salt and pepper. Stir it all up, cover, and cook 3 to 4 hours or until set. ■

This is especially wonderful with Thanksgiving and Christmas dinner (when the oven schedule is tighter than last year's snow pants!) Or, serve it alongside some tasty taco meat and shredded lettuce. Wow! —JS

Jenny Matlock
Mesa, Arizona

Baked Potatoes

Makes 4 to 12 servings

4 to 12 potatoes (1 per serving)
Sea or kosher salt (optional)

Scrub the potatoes thoroughly and poke the skin with a fork in several places. While the potato skin is damp, sprinkle with salt if desired. Wrap each potato tightly in aluminum foil and fill the dry slow cooker with wrapped potatoes. Cover and cook on low for 7 to 9 hours or on high for 3 to 4 hours, until the potatoes are tender. ∎

Although the holidays are wonderful,
my oven is often filled to beyond-full capacity.
Using the slow cooker to cook potatoes frees up space
and gives us a moist, delicious potato every time. —JM

side dishes

Sharon Brown
Mullica Hill, New Jersey

Sweet Potato Puff

Makes 8 servings

Sweet Potato Base

6 medium sweet potatoes or yams (about 3 pounds)

1/2 cup granulated sugar

8 tablespoons (1 stick) butter or margarine, melted

2 eggs, beaten

1/3 cup milk

1 teaspoon maple syrup

Butter-flavored cooking spray

Topping

1/2 cup firmly packed dark brown sugar

2 tablespoons butter or margarine, melted

1/4 cup all-purpose flour

To make the sweet potato base, cook the sweet potatoes in boiling water until tender, about 30 minutes. Cool and peel. Mash the sweet potatoes until no longer lumpy. You should have about 3 cups. In a mixing bowl, beat the potatoes, sugar, melted butter, eggs, milk, and maple syrup until fluffy. Spray the inside of a 5-quart slow cooker

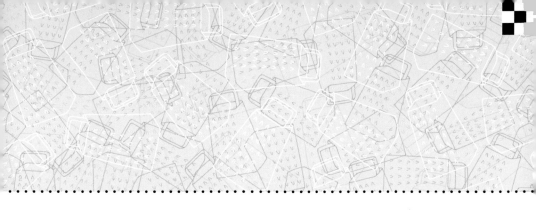

with the cooking spray. Spoon the sweet potato mixture into the slow cooker.

To make the topping, combine the brown sugar, melted butter, and flour until well blended. Sprinkle over the sweet potatoes. Set the slow cooker on low, cover, and cook for 3 to 4 hours or until set and a knife inserted in the center comes out clean.

I have used the slow cooker liner bags. The recipe turns out fine, and the cleanup process for the slow cooker is quick and easy. ■

I was born and grew up in Memphis, Tennessee. I now live in New Jersey, but my love for certain southern foods remains with me. Years ago my mom and I came up with this recipe for sweet potatoes, and it has become a standard for Easter Sunday. As the family has grown to include extended families and grandchildren, this recipe has become the most requested to prepare for showers, christenings, and other social gatherings. —SB

Stephanie Jonker
Shreveport, Louisiana

Raonna's
Mac & Cheese

Makes 8 to 10 servings

1 (16-ounce) package elbow macaroni

4 tablespoons (1/2 stick) butter

Salt and black pepper

1 pound pasturized processed cheese (such as Velveeta), cubed

1/2 pound sharp cheddar cheese, shredded

1 egg, thoroughly beaten

1 tablespoon mustard

1 quart milk, approximately

Cook the macaroni al dente and drain. Spray a 5-quart slow cooker with nonstick spray. While still hot, put it in a slow cooker and stir in the butter until it melts completely. Season with salt and pepper and stir in the cheeses. Combine the beaten egg, mustard, and 2 cups of the milk. Whisk well and pour this mixture over the macaroni and cheese. Pour the other 2 cups of milk over that. Cover and cook on low for 2 to 3 hours, stirring midway through. ■

If you're finishing this at a remote location, you can omit the second addition of milk and just take a 13-ounce can of evaporated milk and pour it in when you turn on the slow cooker. —SJ

Debbie Groff
Ankeny, Iowa

Best-Ever
Macaroni & Cheese

Makes 8 servings

8 ounces macaroni, cooked and drained

1 1/2 cups milk

1 (12-ounce) can evaporated milk

2 eggs, well beaten

2 teaspoons salt

3 cups shredded cheddar cheese

Softened butter or margarine

Combine the cooked macaroni, milk, evaporated milk, eggs, salt, and 2 1/2 cups of the cheese. Heavily grease a 5-quart slow cooker with butter. Turn the macaroni mixture into the slow cooker and top with the remaining 1/2 cup cheese. Cover and cook on low for 2 to 3 hours, stirring midway through. ■

Great to take to potlucks. —DG

side dishes

Mindy Readshaw–Bloomberg
Venetia, Pennsylvania

Mimmy's Apple, Sausage &
Cranberry Stuffing

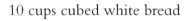

Makes 25 servings

4 cups cubed whole wheat bread

10 cups cubed white bread

2 1/2 pounds bulk sausage

2 cups chopped celery

2 tablespoons chopped fresh sage

1 1/2 tablespoons chopped fresh rosemary

1 teaspoon chopped fresh thyme

3 Golden Delicious apples, cored and chopped (not peeled)

2 cups dried sweetened cranberries

3/4 cup minced fresh Italian (flat-leaf) parsley

2 cups turkey stock, or more if needed

3 eggs

2/3 cup unsalted butter, melted

Preheat the oven to 350°F. Spread the bread cubes in a single layer on a large baking sheet and bake for 5 to 7 minutes, or until evenly toasted. Transfer the toasted bread cubes to a very large baking pan.

In a large skillet, cook the sausage over medium heat, stirring and breaking up the lumps, until browned evenly.

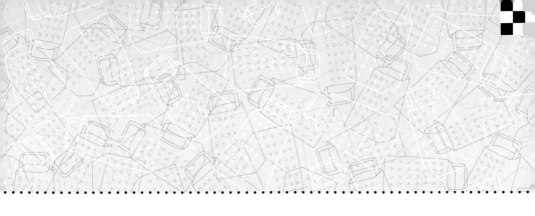

Add the celery, sage, rosemary, and thyme; cook, stirring, for 2 minutes to blend the flavors.

Pour the sausage mixture over the bread. Mix in the chopped apples, dried cranberries, and parsley. Drizzle with the turkey stock, eggs, and melted butter. Mix with your hands. Spray a 6-quart slow cooker with nonstick spray. Place the stuffing in the slow cooker, cover, and cook on low for 5 to 7 hours, stirring midway through cooking. I cook it from about 9:00 in the morning of Thanksgiving Day until dinner at 4:00. If needed, add more both sparingly.

Variations

Try experimenting with different breads and apples. Use pork or turkey sausage, or vegetarian breakfast patties. I prefer the pork sausage. Add pecans too.

You can get this ready to cook the night before. Just omit the broth. The next morning, mix it with the broth and place it in your slow cooker. ∎

side dishes

167

I am not a glutton—
I am an explorer of food.

—Erma Bombeck

Dips & Sauces

Sandy Gratz
Verona, Wisconsin

Mexican Chili Dip

Makes about 3 1/2 cups

1 (8-ounce) package cream cheese, cubed

1 (16-ounce) can chili without beans

1 (4-ounce) can chopped green chiles

1 cup shredded Colby-Jack cheese

1 (4-ounce) can chopped black olives

3 green onions, chopped

Tortilla chips, for dipping

Spray a 2-quart slow cooker with nonstick spray. Combine all ingredients except the chips in the slow cooker, cover, and cook on high for 30 minutes or until the cheese is melted. Stir, then reduce the heat to low. Serve warm with tortilla chips. ∎

This is a family recipe that we found after our mother-in-law died. Everyone loves it, and we think of her every time we make it. —SG

Hannah Anderson
Springfield, Missouri

Spicy Heaven Dip

Makes 6 cups

1 (16-ounce) package hot or spicy bulk sausage

5 (8-ounce) packages cream cheese, or to taste, cubed

1 (10-ounce) can diced tomatoes with green chiles
      (mild or hot as desired), drained, or more to taste

Brown the sausage in a skillet over medium heat, about 15 minutes; drain. Spray a 2-quart slow cooker with nonstick spray. Put all the ingredients in it, cover, and cook on high for 30 minutes to 1 hour until the cream cheese is melted and creamy, stirring midway through. Turn to low for serving, up to 3 hours. ∎

This is a great dip whose taste is underestimated
by the limited number of ingredients.
Once the party has realized how simple and easy it is,
it's a for-sure party favorite. —HA

dips & sauces

Jenny Matlock
Mesa, Arizona

Walnut Butterscotch Dip

Makes 3 1/2 cups

Vegetable oil cooking spray

2 (11-ounce) packages butterscotch-flavored chips

2/3 cup nonfat evaporated milk

2/3 cup finely chopped toasted walnuts

1 tablespoon dark rum or 1 teaspoon rum extract

1/2 teaspoon butter extract

1/8 teaspoon salt

Apple and pear wedges, and pound cake and angel food
cake squares, for serving

Set a 2-quart slow cooker to low. Spray the inside with nonstick spray. Mix the butterscotch chips and evaporated milk together in the slow cooker. Cover and cook on low for 1 to 2 hours, until the chips are melted and smooth, stirring midway through. Stir in the walnuts, extracts, and salt. Cover and continue to cook on low for 15 minutes. The dip can be reheated. Serve with apple and pear wedges, and pound and angel food cake squares. ■

Use any leftovers of this delicious dip over ice cream. —JM

Carrie Shindorf
Cosby, Missouri

Autumn
Caramel Dip

Makes about 2 1/2 cups

4 tablespoons (1/2 stick) butter

1/2 cup light corn syrup

1 cup firmly packed brown sugar

1 (14-ounce) can sweetened condensed milk

Apple slices, for serving

Spray a 2-quart slow cooker with nonstick spray. Mix together all the ingredients except the apples in the cooker. Cover and cook on low for 2 to 3 hours, stirring after 1 hour. Dip fresh apple slices into the hot caramel dip! ∎

As a home school family, each fall we would head to Jones Orchard for our September field trip. We would be greeted by Mrs. Jones in her bonnet. She was such a cute grandmother type who always remembered us from the year before. Before we left for our outing I would prepare this family favorite. After a fun morning of picking our apples and visiting with Mrs. Jones we would head home for our wonderful caramel dip and apples. What wonderful memories this recipe will create! —CS

dips & sauces

Kathy Tanner
Bellevue, Washington

Rhubarb Sauce

Makes about 2 cups

4 cups sliced rhubarb (about 1-inch pieces)

1/2 cup firmly packed brown sugar

1/2 teaspoon ground cinnamon

1/4 teaspoon ground cardamom

Mix everything in a 2-quart slow cooker, cover, and cook on low for 4 hours. ■

This is such a simple way to use rhubarb
over ice cream, yogurt, or granola.
No mess, no watched pot.
Make it ahead of time and you can relax later. —KT

Martha Locke
Dallas, Texas

Bodacious
Vodka Sauce

Makes about 10 cups

1 large sweet onion, finely chopped

5 cloves garlic, finely chopped

3 tablespoons extra virgin olive oil

2 (28-ounce) cans crushed tomatoes, with liquid

1 1/4 cups vodka

2 cups heavy cream

1/4 cup chopped fresh basil leaves

1/4 cup chopped fresh thyme leaves

1 (12-ounce) can tomato paste, or to taste

Sauté the onion and garlic in the olive oil in a large saucepan over medium heat until translucent, about 5 minutes. Transfer to a 5-quart slow cooker. Add the crushed tomatoes, vodka, heavy cream, basil, and thyme. Add the tomato paste by spoonfuls until it reaches the desired consistency. Cover and cook on low for 5 to 6 hours. Great over pasta with freshly grated Parmesan. ■

My family always gets to choose what they would like to have for their birthday dinner, and this is chosen more times than not. You can substitute 8 to 12 fresh tomatoes for the canned, or enough to make about 5 cups. —ML

dips & sauces

175

Cathy Jackson
Iona, Idaho

Garden
Spaghetti Sauce

Makes about 14 cups

1 pound ground beef

2 (28-ounce) cans whole peeled tomatoes, with liquid

1 (6-ounce) can tomato paste

2 to 3 cloves garlic, peeled

1 1/2 teaspoons dried oregano leaves

1 1/2 teaspoons dried basil leaves

1/8 teaspoon hot red pepper flakes

1 teaspoon sugar

2 to 3 tablespoons olive oil, to taste

2 tablespoons freshly shredded Parmesan cheese

Salt and black pepper

1 green bell pepper, diced

1 small onion, diced

1 1/2 cups diced celery

1 pound fresh mushrooms, sliced

Brown the ground beef in a skillet over medium-high heat, 8 to 10 minutes; drain. Put the canned tomatoes, tomato paste, and garlic in a blender and process until blended well. You may need to do this in two batches to avoid overflow. Put into a 6-quart slow cooker and stir in the

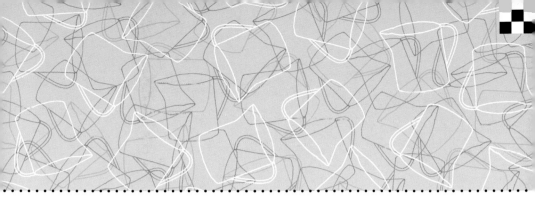

oregano, basil, red pepper flakes, sugar, olive oil, Parmesan, and salt and pepper to taste. Add the green pepper, onion, celery, and mushrooms, stirring them into the sauce. Add the ground beef, stirring it into the sauce. Cover and cook on low for 6 to 8 hours. Serve over your favorite cooked pasta. ∎

The family loves this spaghetti sauce with the addition of the vegetables and the rich, robust flavor it has after it's simmered all day long in the slow cooker. Serve it over a whole-grain pasta for an even healthier meal.
Leave out the vegetables and the ground beef and cook on low in the slow cooker for about 4 hours or on the stove for 20 to 30 minutes.
It's a wonderful marinara sauce for dipping or eating over pasta.
I also use this sauce minus the vegetables for lasagna and then cooked on the stove for 20 to 30 minutes.
A very versatile recipe. —CJ

dips & sauces

Debra Fricano
Aiea, Hawaii

Deb's Sweet "Hot"
Pasta Sauce

Makes about 9 cups

2 tablespoons olive oil, or more as needed

1 (12-ounce) bag frozen soy crumbles or 1 pound ground
    meat of your choice

1 medium onion, chopped

1 medium red bell pepper, chopped

1 medium yellow or green bell pepper, chopped

1 pound cremini or shiitake mushrooms, sliced

2 cloves garlic, chopped

1 teaspoon hot red pepper flakes

1/4 teaspoon ground black pepper

1/4 teaspoon salt or low-salt seasoning blend

2 bay leaves

3 (8-ounce) cans low- or no-sodium tomato sauce

1 (6-ounce) can tomato paste, or less, depending on how
    thick you want your sauce

2 cups water

1/4 to 1/2 cup fudge sauce

Warm the olive oil in a 4-quart Dutch oven or saucepan over medium heat. Add the soy crumbles, onion, bell peppers, mushrooms, garlic, red pepper flakes, pepper, and salt to

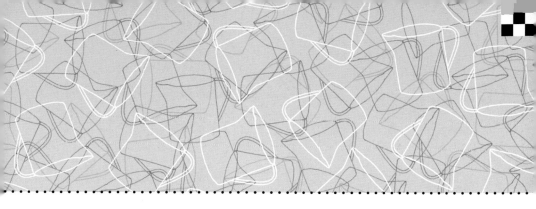

the saucepan. Cook until the onion is translucent, 5 to 10 minutes. Place in a 5-quart slow cooker and add the bay leaves, tomato sauce, tomato paste, and water. Cover and cook on low for 6 to 8 hours. Stir in the fudge sauce during the last 10 minutes. Discard the bay leaves. Serve over the pasta of your choice. ■

This was my mom's and maternal grandmother's spaghetti sauce. Over the years I have added my own twists to it. I use it for many things. I use it in my lasagna recipe, my chili recipes, and over pastas with a twist. My mom and grandmother were great cooks, and I loved working in the kitchen with them. I have always loved the smell of a good spaghetti sauce cooking over the stove or in a slow cooker. It makes me remember my mom and grandmother fondly. I add fudge sauce to my recipe to give it just a bit of a sweet flavor, but not too sweet. It counteracts the acidity from the tomato sauce. I have made it healthier over the years by using frozen soy crumbles or ground turkey breast. —DF

dips & sauces

Life is uncertain.
Eat dessert first.

—Ernestine Ulmer

Desserts

Elizabeth Listello
Grand Rapids, Michigan

Indian Corn Pudding

Makes 6 generous servings

1 1/2 cups cold milk

1 cup cornmeal

3 cups scalded milk (skim works fine), still hot

1/2 cup molasses

1 teaspoon salt

1/2 cup sugar

3/4 teaspoon ground ginger

1/4 teaspoon freshly grated nutmeg

4 tablespoons (1/2 stick) butter

Mix 1 cup of the cold milk with the cornmeal, then stir into the hot milk in the saucepan. Heat very slowly on low, stirring for 10 to 15 minutes, until thick. Mix in the molasses, salt, sugar, ginger, nutmeg, and butter. Pour into a buttered 4-quart slow cooker. Pour the remaining cold milk into the center and stir. Cover and cook on low for 3 1/2 to 4 1/2 hours, depending on the consistency you prefer. Cool slightly before serving. ■

My mother visited New England in the 1970s and brought this recipe home. We've adjusted it over the years. It's a Thanksgiving tradition. —EL

Sue Welch
Kaysville, Utah

Chocolate Cake

Dessert

Makes 8 to 10 servings

1 (12-ounce) bag semisweet chocolate chips

1 (3.4-ounce) package instant chocolate pudding mix

1 cup sour cream

1 (18.25-ounce) box chocolate cake mix, batter prepared
according to package instructions

Butter-flavored cooking spray

Vanilla ice cream, for serving

Stir the chocolate chips, pudding mix, and sour cream into the prepared cake batter. Spray a 3-quart or larger slow cooker with butter-flavored cooking spray, and then pour the batter into it. Cover and cook on high for about 2 hours, and then stir well. Cover and cook on high for another 1 1/2 hours or until the dessert is mostly set in the middle and firm around the edges. The top and middle will still be a little gooey. Turn off the slow cooker and let it sit for at least 30 minutes. The dessert will have the consistency of a bread pudding. Spoon it into bowls and serve with vanilla ice cream. ■

desserts

Sue Welch
Kaysville, Utah

Lemon Cake

Dessert

Makes 8 to 10 servings

1 (12-ounce) bag white chocolate chips

1 (3.4-ounce) package instant lemon pudding mix

1 cup sour cream

1 (18.25-ounce) box lemon cake mix, batter prepared
     according to package instructions

Butter-flavored cooking spray

Vanilla ice cream, for serving

Stir the white chocolate chips, pudding mix, and sour cream into the prepared cake batter. Spray a 3-quart or larger slow cooker with butter-flavored cooking spray, and then pour the batter into it. Cover and cook on high for about 2 hours, and then stir well. Cover and cook on high for another 1 1/2 hours or until the dessert is mostly set in the middle and firm around the edges. The top and middle will still be a little gooey. Turn off the slow cooker and let it sit for at least 30 minutes. The dessert will have the consistency of a bread pudding. Spoon it into bowls and serve with vanilla ice cream. ■

Michele Jewell
Gettysburg, Pennsylvania

Carrot Cake
Dessert

Makes 6 to 8 servings

Vegetable oil cooking spray or vegetable oil

1 (18.25-ounce) box spice cake mix

1 (3.4-ounce) box instant butterscotch pudding mix

1 cup water

2 cups finely shredded carrots

3/4 cup canola oil

4 eggs

1 (8-ounce) can crushed pineapple, with liquid

1 cup sour cream

Spray a 3- to 6-quart slow cooker with cooking spray or oil it lightly. Combine the rest of the ingredients in a bowl and beat on medium speed for 2 minutes. Pour the mixture into the cooker. Cover and cook on high for 2 1/2 to 3 hours or until the dessert is spongy in the middle and the edges are golden brown. The texture will be like that of a soft bread pudding. Turn off the cooker and let it sit for 20 minutes, then spoon the dessert into bowls and serve warm. ∎

desserts

Paula Kerr
Sherwood, Arkansas

Sweet & Simple
Applesauce Pie

Makes 6 servings

1/2 cup plus 2 tablespoons sugar

Ground cinnamon for sprinkling

1 prepared piecrust

10 to 15 medium Granny Smith apples

1 cup red-hot candies

1/2 cup water

Sprinkle the 2 tablespoons of sugar and a dusting of cinnamon on top of the piecrust. Bake at 375°F until golden, 15 to 20 minutes. Let cool, then break into pieces into 6 dessert dishes. Peel, core, and slice the apples and place in a 5-quart slow cooker. Pour the red-hots, water, and remaining sugar on top. Cover and cook on low for 5 to 7 hours, stirring occasionally. When the apples have completely cooked down, mash them into a slightly chunky applesauce. Spoon the mixture on top of the piecrust pieces. Garnish with a dash of cinnamon and serve warm. ∎

As a kindergarten teacher, I focused each September on a study of apples and culminated with this sweet recipe. My students would even take turns peeling apples with an old-fashioned crank peeler. —PK

Glenda DePugh
St. Joseph, Missouri

Hot Holiday Punch

Makes 15 to 20 servings

2 quarts water

1 quart cranberry juice

2 cups sugar

2 cups orange juice

1 tablespoon fresh lemon juice

2 cups pineapple juice

3 whole cinnamon sticks

1 tablespoon whole cloves

Set a 6-quart slow cooker on high. Add the water and cranberry juice. When hot, about 2 to 3 hours, add the sugar and stir until dissolved. Add the remaining ingredients. Turn the heat to low and simmer 2 to 5 hours, the longer the better. I fix it around midmorning and let it simmer on low all day and into the evening. That way it is hot and available for guests to enjoy anytime. It also gives your house a wonderful "Holiday aroma." It can be stored in the refrigerator for up to two weeks and reheated. ■

I have been making this recipe at Christmastime for the past twenty-five years. I hope your family enjoys it, too! —GDP

desserts

Metric Conversions & Equivalents

Approximate Metric Equivalents

Volume

1/4 teaspoon = 1 milliliter
1/2 teaspoon = 2.5 milliliters
3/4 teaspoon = 4 milliliters
1 teaspoon = 5 milliliters
1 1/4 teaspoons = 6 milliliters
1 1/2 teaspoons = 7.5 milliliters
1 3/4 teaspoons = 8.5 milliliters
2 teaspoons = 10 milliliters
1 tablespoon (1/2 fluid ounce) = 15 milliliters
2 tablespoons (1 fluid ounce) = 30 milliliters
1/4 cup = 60 milliliters
1/3 cup = 80 milliliters
1/2 cup (4 fluid ounces) = 120 milliliters
2/3 cup = 160 milliliters
3/4 cup = 180 milliliters
1 cup (8 fluid ounces) = 240 milliliters
1 1/4 cups = 300 milliliters
1 1/2 cups (12 fluid ounces) = 360 milliliters
1 2/3 cups = 400 milliliters
2 cups (1 pint) = 460 milliliters
3 cups = 700 milliliters
4 cups (1 quart) = 0.95 liter
1 quart plus 1/4 cup = 1 liter
4 quarts (1 gallon) = 3.8 liters

Weight

1/4 ounce = 7 grams

1/2 ounce = 14 grams

3/4 ounce = 21 grams

1 ounce = 28 grams

1 1/4 ounces = 35 grams

1 1/2 ounces = 42.5 grams

1 2/3 ounces = 45 grams

2 ounces = 57 grams

3 ounces = 85 grams

4 ounces (1/4 pound) = 113 grams

5 ounces = 142 grams

6 ounces = 170 grams

7 ounces = 198 grams

8 ounces (1/2 pound) = 227 grams

16 ounces (1 pound) = 454 grams

35.25 ounces (2.2 pounds) = 1 kilogram

Length

1/8 inch = 3 millimeters

1/4 inch = 6 millimeters

1/2 inch = 1.25 centimeters

1 inch = 2.5 centimeters

2 inches = 5 centimeters

2 1/2 inches = 6 centimeters

4 inches = 10 centimeters

5 inches = 13 centimeters

6 inches = 15.25 centimeters

12 inches (1 foot) = 30 centimeters

Information compiled from a variety of sources, including *Recipes into Type* by
Joan Whitman and Dolores Simon (Newton, MA: Biscuit Books, 2000); *The New
Food Lover's Companion* by Sharon Tyler Herbst (Hauppauge, NY: Barron's, 1995);
and *Rosemary Brown's Big Kitchen Instruction Book* (Kansas City, MO:
Andrews McMeel, 1998).

Metric Conversion Formulas

To Convert	Multiply
Ounces to grams	Ounces by 28.35
Pounds to kilograms	Pounds by 0.454
Teaspoons to milliliters	Teaspoons by 4.93
Tablespoons to milliliters	Tablespoons by 14.79
Fluid ounces to milliliters	Fluid ounces by 29.57
Cups to milliliters	Cups by 236.59
Cups to liters	Cups by 0.236
Pints to liters	Pints by 0.473
Quarts to liters	Quarts by 0.946
Gallons to liters	Gallons by 3.785
Inches to centimeters	Inches by 2.54

Oven Temperatures

To convert Fahrenheit to Celsius, subtract 32 from Fahrenheit, multiply the result by 5, then divide by 9.

Description	Fahrenheit	Celsius	British Gas Mark
Very cool	200°	95°	0
Very cool	225°	110°	1/4
Very cool	250°	120°	1/2
Cool	275°	135°	1
Cool	300°	150°	2
Warm	325°	165°	3
Moderate	350°	175°	4
Moderately hot	375°	190°	5
Fairly hot	400°	200°	6
Hot	425°	220°	7
Very hot	450°	230°	8
Very hot	475°	245°	9

Common Ingredients & Their Approximate Equivalents

1 cup uncooked rice = 225 grams

1 cup all-purpose flour = 140 grams

1 stick butter (4 ounces • 1/2 cup • 8 tablespoons) = 110 grams

1 cup butter (8 ounces • 2 sticks • 16 tablespoons) = 220 grams

1 cup brown sugar, firmly packed = 225 grams

1 cup granulated sugar = 200 grams

Index